The
FRAGRANT
YEAR

The
FRAGRANT
YEAR

Growing and using scented flowers
all year round

Jane Newdick

With photography by Pia Tryde

Little, Brown and Company
Boston • Toronto • London

A LITTLE, BROWN BOOK

This edition first published in 1993

ISBN 0-316-90524-0
A CIP catalogue record for this book is available from the British Library.

AN EDDISON·SADD EDITION
Edited, designed and produced by
Eddison Sadd Editions Limited
St Chad's Court
146B King's Cross Road
London WC1X 9DH

Phototypeset in Stempel Garamond by
SX Composing Ltd, Rayleigh, England
Colour originated in Kuala Lumpur, Malaysia
Printed and bound by Artes Graficas Toledo, SA in Spain
DLTO: 2110-1992

Little, Brown and Company (UK) Ltd
165 Great Dover Street
London SE1 4YA

Page 1 *Warmed by bright spring sunshine, tulips open their petals wide
and the hyacinths and wallflowers release their scent into the air.
These three varieties of plant are a classic choice for planting into tubs
and containers.*

Pages 2-3 *Glistening, white* longiflorum *lilies combine with white
honesty flowers and pale, waxy tulips in a tall arrangement. These
lilies are traditionally used as an Easter decoration.*

CONTENTS

Introduction

THE
FRAGRANT
GARDEN

The best way to enjoy the many fragrances to be discovered in the natural world is through a small garden of your own. This may be anything from just a single pot or small courtyard to vast, spreading acres. Whatever size it is, let it provide scented plants through the seasons to fill the house with fragrance or simply to surround you with their garden scents as they grow.

The soft, violet-pink blooms of the 'Hagley Hybrid' clematis clamber through the small, scented-flowered shrub, Philadelphus coronarius 'Variegatus', providing contrast and definition among the cream-edged leaves.

The idea of a garden as a place that pleases all our senses is not new. It has been understood and practised for as long as man has grown plants with no particular value as a food crop. From the very earliest times, when men settled, built communities and farmed, gardens have been created simply for their delight. Extravagant gardens were designed as a show of wealth for royalty and powerful, influential people. Monastic and other religious communities grew plants in their gardens for their herbal and medicinal uses as well as creating places for contemplative study.

As plants were collected from the wild to grow in gardens and then improved upon by selective breeding and hybridization, fragrance was nearly always a special consideration. Nowadays, however, in our bland, technological age we are less conscious perhaps of the natural scents around us. We are assailed by harsh, powerful, artificial aromas from the chemists' laboratories as well as the scents that are a side-effect of the way we choose to live. Where once there was the smell of animals, we now have the smell of engine exhaust emissions; the 'green' scents of forests and meadows have been replaced by factory fumes and burning fuels. We can still create small oases of scent, however, if we have a garden or even just a room to call our own.

Most gardens are small these days so every plant grown in them should earn its keep. If a flower or leaf is good to look at and good to smell then it deserves a space. Many scented plants retain their fragrance even after they are dried; others give up their scent in some way so that it can be stored or used to perfume something else and enjoyed long after the plant has died. Ways and means of doing this have been perfected over the centuries. In many cases it is as simple as mixing petals and leaves with spices and substances that will fix the scent, or infusing the fresh flowers in a liquid to make anything from a soothing lotion to a delicious drink. Two powerfully evocative flowers, the rose and the lily, have become icons of scent as well as having a wealth of symbolic meanings. They are grown and appreciated as widely today as they ever were in ancient times and prove that there are parts of our natural world that remain deeply woven into our human consciousness. Alongside these two flowers are thousands of different scented plants with perfumes ranging from cool and sharp citrus scents to warm and spicy clove scents. Perfume is contained in the flowers, leaves, roots, stems and fruits. Sometimes it is so volatile that it carries on the air for long distances; at other times it is locked deep within the plant and only released by crushing, grinding or even drying the plant.

THE SCIENCE AND ART OF SCENT

Fragrance, by its nature, is very difficult to write about. It is possible to discuss it in completely scientific terms using chemical symbols and names for substances, and to describe the effect it has on people

in a biological way. There is so much more to it than this, however. Although it is vital to understand what it is, how it is made and why it exists, scent has an effect on us that goes further than mere biology. It can profoundly affect how we feel, both physically and mentally. It is completely bound up with how we taste food and drink and it can stir ancient memories, be evocative of place and time, soothe us, comfort us, even disturb and distress us. We can be attracted or repelled by certain scents and each of us has different preferences and dislikes as well as varying degrees of sensitivity to smells. Plant fragrances are generally present for a botanical purpose and their effect on humans is simply a consequence of us having a fairly acute sense of smell. In the animal kingdom, though, the human capability to sense smell is extremely feeble compared with many species. It may well be growing less and less important as we evolve and develop and hardly need it at all as a sense for survival.

Nowadays we can accurately copy and manufacture many natural scents as well as produce many blends and new fragrances in the laboratory. We use artificial fragrances for all kinds of products, from washing powders and air fresheners to fuels. The substance that gives a specific flower or plant its perfume identity can be isolated and re-created so that perfumes that would cost enormous sums of money to extract from plants can be made simply in a test tube. The perfume industry flourishes by making new scents for every decade that passes, yet the old, favourite fragrances based on flowers still

An old orchard in full bloom filled with the scent of apple blossom and the soft background hum of foraging insects and bees. At this time of year, even bare earth and new grass seem to smell delicious and fresh throughout the garden.

remain popular and are used in many perfumes.

We have lost the sense of the perfume of plants being a mystical and magical thing since chemistry has explained what fragrance really is. The medieval gardener thought that the fragrance from flowers was God's breath on Earth and treated it with appropriate reverence. Enclosed scented gardens were created specially for pleasure and contemplation, as places in which to walk or sit quietly, just as they had been from the earliest times in places such as ancient Greece, Egypt, Persia, India and China.

Scents for survival

Plants produce perfume to ensure their own survival, both as a means of protection against predators and to attract insect pollinators. The essential oils made in the foliage of scented-leaved plants are generally there to ward off animals and insects that might otherwise eat them. Many aromatic herbs that live in arid conditions are protected from drying out by the oily vapour given off by the leaves. The oils obtained from scented leaves generally have antiseptic properties, which have long been made use of by humans. These are simply a protection for the plant when damaged. The early plants that colonized the Earth, such as conifers, were wind-fertilized, as there were few flying insects, and the sticky, aromatic gum the trees produced meant that damage to the bark was quickly healed over by the resinous coating.

Lilac is grown commercially as a cut flower and often forced for earlier flowering. These branches, complete with generous foliage, have been picked from a garden that has plenty to spare.

Flowers fertilized by moths and butterflies are the most strongly scented as they have to attract the flying insects from great distances. The most fragrant of all are the night-flowering plants usually found growing in shady places, with pale or white flowers designed to attract moths such as hawk-moths. The flowers of these plants are generally tubular in shape and can therefore only offer nectar to insects with very long tongues. They usually bloom only for one night, opening as the air cools and dying the next day. The majority of these night-scented plants grow in tropical regions or in sheltered, wooded conditions where moths abound. There are few scented flowers of this kind growing in Canada, New Zealand and the Arctic regions, where the Lepidoptera (moths and butterflies) are unable to survive the unfavourable climatic conditions.

Bees find flowers from which to feed by sight, not smell, and are always attracted by blue flowers, though other signs and distinguishing marks play an important part too. Little marks or lines on the petals or the central yellow eye of a flower are the guides to pollination, which for the plant's benefit must be done quickly and accurately. Bees can feed from tubular and lipped flowers. In cool climates, they are the most important plant pollinators. Few of the flowers pollinated by bees need to be scented and it seems that where colour is intensified in a flower, the scent diminishes. Many autumn-flowering plants, for example, are highly coloured but lack scent in their flowers. Families of flowers, such as the poppy, which are nearly all self-pollinating, have no need of scent and are generally known for the brilliance and range of their colours. Two types from cool climatic regions possess a little scent, *Papaver nudicaule* or Iceland poppy, and the tree poppy *Romneya coulteri*, which both happen to need the help of insects for fertilization.

Classifying scents

The olfactory system is thought to be the most primitive of all our senses and the one we most neglect. We sense smell through tiny rods covered in olfactory hairs that project into the mucous membrane at the top of our nose. The ends of these tiny hairs taper into nerve fibres, which are in direct contact with the central nervous system. It takes 0.5 of a second to register a scent compared with 0.9 of a second to register pain or 0.15 to register sound. When we eat or drink we open our mouth and any aroma is taken up into the nose so that taste, or our perception of taste, is in fact a subtle interaction of the registering of smell and basic taste, which comprises sweet, salt and bitter.

Certain scents can become unpleasant after prolonged exposure to them although they may start off as a delicious perfume. This can be because a scent is too powerful or concentrated or at too close a range. Often it is because the perfume is over-sweet and contains the substance indole. Present in flowers such as the narcissus and the lily, it is very like the animal perfume obtained from the civet, which is also present in the putrefaction of animal tissue. If a scent is heavy, sickly and very sweet, indole is likely to be present. The scent of violets has a strange quality. After prolonged exposure to it the olfactory nerves become tired causing the perfume to fade. It is as if the nose has been anaesthetized and has to rest before being able to appreciate the scent again. This effect is caused by an organic compound called a ketone. In violets, the type of ketone present is called ionone. Orris root contains a similar substance, irone, which gives the rhizome its violet-like perfume. Other powerful flower scents were once believed to send people to sleep or even cause madness. There is no doubt that perfume can have a powerful effect on the human body.

The subtlety of a flower scent relies upon the chemical compound mix within the essential oil contained in the leaf or flower. The type of alcohol within the essential oil determines a flower's characteristic scent and the combination of acid and alcohol makes the commonest compound, known as an ester. The different alcohols in essential oils have names such as geraniol, borneol, which is the chief alcohol in leaves, and menthol, eucalyptol and linalol. Essential oils are soluble only in alcohol and this was not discovered until the end of the fourteenth century. It means that the extraction of the oils is a difficult and usually costly process. An alcoholic solution of essential oil is known as an essence and a flower essential oil is called an attar, or otto, from an old Persian word meaning 'scent'. Essential oils are contained in different parts of flowers and leaves, making some easier to extract than others. In bay and myrtle leaves the scent is embedded deep within the leaf tissue and can only be smelt after strongly squeezing or bruising the leaf. Other plants though, such as thyme and many heat-loving aromatic herbs, release their scent easily from their leaves as they are warmed by the sun and other sources of warmth.

The perfume industry describes flower fragrances using a musical metaphor. There are three separate notes that together make a chord. The top note, or impact note, is registered first by the nose, sometimes with surprise. The middle note is the next one to be detected and develops into the lasting, true fragrance. Finally, there is a base or bottom note, which becomes more obvious as the scent fades or as one moves away from the source. Few flowers produce a simple, single note of fragrance as they are invariably made up of complex mixtures of chemicals. Scents affect the olfactory nerves according to their volatility and all fragrances have different rates at which they evaporate. Strong scents, such as cedar and clove, have a very low volatility while those with a high volatility, such as citron and bergamot, are considered weak or feeble scents, obvious at first but weakening rapidly.

The eighteenth-century Swedish naturalist, Carl Linnaeus, made a crude attempt to categorize flower fragrances. He came up with the descriptions aromatic, alliaceous (or garlic-smelling), hircine (goat-like), ambrosiac, fragrant and foul or nauseous. The first attempt at a proper classification of flower scents was made by Count von Marilaun in 1893, who divided them into six main groups according to their predominating chemical substance. This has since been further divided to give ten main groups but they have never been officially recognized. They are useful, though, when trying to describe and identify flower scents and perfumes, both artificial and natural, and there are also classifications for leaf fragrances and scents from wood, bark and roots.

Flower scents

1 AMINOID GROUP

This group contains mainly cream or white flowers that grow in dense clusters of many small blooms. The scent is rather unpleasant as the substance indole is contained within the essential oil. An almost ammonia-like tone accompanies a faint fishy aroma. Trees such as sorbus and pyracantha and many of the Umbelliferae family of plants have these flowers. The scent attracts flies for pollination.

2 ANIMAL-SCENTED GROUP

Plants in this group are often also linked with the fruit-scented group. Examples of animal-scented flowers are hypericum, which smells of goat, and Crown Imperial or *Fritillaria imperialis*, which smells of fox. Valerian and ox-eye daisy are also included, containing the unpleasant-smelling substance, valeric acid, which is also present in human perspiration. Plants with a musk scent are also in this group.

3 AROMATIC GROUP

This is a lovely group of scents containing all the spicy fragrances, such as clove, cinnamon, vanilla, balsam and almond. Flowers such as sweet peas, acacia and bean have a vanilla-and-lemon perfume with a hint of spice when the scent is warm. Eugonol is the essential oil found in clove and it is present in stocks, carnations and pinks as well as peonies and *Viburnum carlesii*. Heliotrope and *Convolvulus arvensis*, the pretty, wild field weed with pink and white stripes, have a distinct almond fragrance.

4 FRUIT-SCENTED GROUP

Another wonderful group containing all the fruit scents except citrus. There are the fresh, apple scents of sweetbriar, the warm, orange scents of philadelphus and some roses such as the climber 'Seagull', and the refreshing pineapple fragrance of pineapple sage and *Cytisus battandieri*. Other fruit scents, such as apricot, plum, even banana and coconut, are perceptible in many flowers.

5 HEAVY GROUP

Flower scents in this group are related to the aminoid group as the essential oil contains indole. The overall scent is sweeter and less concentrated, and therefore only unpleasant when the fragrance is inhaled for too long or smelt at too close a range. Many of the flowers in this group have what is called a 'tropical' perfume and are invariably white or cream in colour. Included are narcissus, *Lilium candidum*, syringas (lilac), tuberose, eucharis and philadelphus. From a distance, the scents of all these flowers are appealing, but in a confined space they can become sickly and overpowering.

6 HONEY GROUP

As the name suggests, this group includes flowers with a sweet scent, such as buddleia, honeysuckle, clover and sedum, all loved by butterflies and nectar-seeking insects. This group is closely related to the animal-scent group and overlaps in some species.

7 INDOLOID GROUP

This is another unpleasant group of scents belonging to such plants as arums, stapelia, voodoo lily and skunk-cabbage. Many plants in this category use their fetid scent as a means of attracting insects for pollination. Their colouring is often in the brown and purple range to add visual emphasis to the smell of decayed meat. Interesting, but definitely not for the scented garden.

8 LEMON GROUP

A delicious and refreshing scent, which is easily recognizable and always well loved. This is more commonly a category for leaves rather than flowers though many rose varieties have a lemon tinge to their perfume. Citrus plants themselves are part of this group as are *Aloysia triphylla*, lemon thyme, lemon balm and some pelargoniums and flowers including waterlilies and the magnificent blooms of *Magnolia grandiflora*.

9 ROSE GROUP

This is one of the most pleasant groups, including all the roses and several other plants. Rose scent is rarely overpowering or sickly but always soothing and yet uplifting. The essential oil is geraniol, which is also found in the rose-scented geranium, and it is from this plant that a cheap substitute for pure attar of roses is obtained. The distillation of real rose oil is extremely costly, taking 2000 roses to produce 1 gram of attar. Many rose fragrances have other fruit scents combined with them, ranging from raspberry, through lemon and apricot to spice.

10 VIOLET GROUP

As the name suggests, this group includes violets, but it also contains other plants, such as mignonette, *Iris reticulata*, some acacias and *leucojum vernum*, and the root of the *Iris florentina*. The violet perfume quickly tires the nose and the scent is perceived to fade. The flowers are self-pollinating and so do not have to attract insects.

The violet and viola families are very ancient in garden-history terms. Throughout the centuries they have had periods of intense popularity and then relative obscurity. Scented violets in particular seem due for a garden revival but from a one-time list of 278 scented cultivars it is difficult to find 13 still available.

Leaf scents

Although many leaf scents can be categorized under the list of flower scents, there are four main leaf scents, which cover most fragrant leaves: turpentine, camphor and eucalyptus, menthol, and sulphur. Many fragrant leaves have far more straightforward scents than flowers. Others contain substances not found in flowers and therefore offer some unusual and rare scents. The essential oils are stored in small cells, which are sometimes obvious on the surface of the leaf. Drying leaves tends to intensify their scent; flowers, on the other hand, generally lose their pungency as they wither and age.

Wood, bark and roots

There are two main classifications for the scents of wood, bark and roots: turpentine and aromatic. There is also a rose category for subjects such as the rose-root or *Sedum rhodiola*, a cottage-garden plant from which a simple but fragrant rose-water was once made. The bark of the trees *Pistacia lentiscus* and *P. terebinthus* is used to make turpentine. Obviously, it falls into the first category, along with many conifers that have the scent of turpentine, including Scots pine and cypress. The second aromatic group includes plants such as sassafras and *Cinnamomum camphora* from which camphor can be extracted.

The icy-white bells of snowdrops pierce through dead winter leaves. Their scent is soft, mossy and fleeting. It is worth picking a posy of them to bring indoors in order to study their fine structure and subtle markings and to try to capture a breath of their fragrance.

Essential oil extraction

The extraction of essential oils from plants has been practised for centuries. The earliest perfumes of all seem to have been resin-based scents, such as myrrh and frankincense. They were mainly used for religious ceremony, literally burnt offerings of incense. This was common practice in many religions world-wide. The word perfume is actually derived from the Latin *per* meaning 'through' and *fumare* meaning 'to smoke'. Rose-water is thought to have been first made in tenth-century Persia and by then was probably used as a medicine, cosmetic and ingredient for the kitchen. Throughout history perfumes have had a variety of uses. Today they have acquired the status of a luxury item, used mainly for personal pleasure, though the whole area of therapeutic and healing use has recently opened up again with the growth of interest in aromatherapy. It seems that our ancestors may have known more than us about the properties of plants and their perfumes.

Some oils can be extracted by distillation. Distillation should be used only for plants that can withstand the heat of boiling water without altering their scent. Roses and orange blossom are both suitable for this method as are many barks and wood from trees. This method involves subjecting the blooms to a steam jet which, when condensed, holds the precious oil to be drawn off later.

Another method, extraction, involves washing the flowers or leaves repeatedly in a special petroleum–ether solution until it takes up all the scent. The resulting substance is then washed with alcohol, which is then removed by distillation, leaving behind the pure essential oil.

Enfleurage is a costly and labour-intensive method. It uses the fresh blooms of flowers that would lose their scent if heated. Flowers such as violet, jasmine and lily of the valley are treated in this way. Trays of the blooms are stacked in layers between animal fat. The flowers are changed daily until the fat is laden with scent. Finally the scent is extracted from the fat with alcohol.

Expression is a fairly crude process of extraction suitable for material such as citrus fruit peels as their oils (zest) are near the surface in little capsules. They are crushed between rollers and the oils are washed out, to be separated by extraction later.

All these processes are difficult to create at home, though one can sometimes come across old recipes for layering jasmine blossom in fat or soaking blooms in oiled muslin then wringing out the resulting fragrance. It is far better to buy good, commercially extracted oils and use home-grown flowers and leaves for other scented products.

This book shows you how to bring fragrance into your garden and home throughout the whole year by growing and using scented plants. Even the smallest garden can find room for an aromatic foliage plant or two, or perhaps a sweetly scented climbing rose or neat bush of lavender. If you have no outdoor space at all then plant scented, flowering bulbs to fill the house with fragrance during the coldest, greyest months of the year; or train small pots of jasmine or stephanotis to decorate a bleak outlook from a window. Flowers and leaves you have grown yourself make the sweetest dried mixtures and scented powders, but there are still plenty of projects and gifts to be made using essential oils and other bought ingredients, which are becoming more easily obtainable these days. *The Fragrant Year* suggests, season by season, what to grow, what to pick and the best ways to use your plants. There are recipes and easy instructions to follow and ideas and inspiration to copy, which all combine to make a feast of fragrance, month after month.

Spring
THE
YEAR UNFOLDS

The scents of spring are fresh and invigorating and somehow perfectly in tune with the bright greens, yellows and whites of the flowers, foliage and new grass of the season. Although temperatures outdoors give little opportunity to linger among the garden fragrances, there is plenty to bring indoors and enjoy.

By late spring there are abundant flowers to choose from for indoor arrangements. Many of the most highly scented flowers are white. This collection includes Pheasant's Eye narcissi and branches of delicate white lilac, combining scent and texture.

SWEET-SCENTED BULBS

The welcome flowers of spring bulbs are not only beautiful to look at but Nature has also provided most of them with delicious scents. Jonquils and hyacinths burst with fragrance while many of the more subtly-flowered bulbs have delicate scents to match.

Bulbs are ideal for filling tubs and window-boxes to provide a flash of colour and a lift to the spirits but we are not likely to sit outside amongst them unless the weather is uncharacteristically mild. Brought indoors, though, either as cut flowers or as growing plants, they fill a room with their scents. This is when a little time spent planting and preparing indoor bulbs during the early autumn really pays off. With some juggling you can have a sequence of flowers over several weeks. If you have not got around to planting your own bulbs it is possible to buy small pots of single flowering bulbs that can be potted up into groups or replanted into interesting containers such as baskets.

Growing bulbs look best in as natural a setting as possible, as if you have just dug them out of the ground. Their appearance nearly always benefits from some moss over the soil in the top of the pot or a sprinkling of small pebbles or grit over the surface.

Hyacinths

When planted in containers or on a small scale, groups of hyacinths look best when they are the same colour. In a garden, on a larger scale, a range of colours might work well but when only a few flowers are used together and colour choices are limited, sticking to one is best. A large planting of shades of blue, for example, could look lovely but you would need to have at least ten bulbs for it to look really effective and this would demand a very large container.

The bulbs that have been stored away and then kept cool but light are at last ready to be enjoyed in a warmer part of the house.

Antique hyacinth glasses in jewel colours present the flowering bulb in a spectacular way. Choose the colour of bloom to suit its container. Here, aquamarine blue perfectly sets off shocking pink.

There is a large range of hyacinth colours to choose from these days, though the traditional blues, pinks and whites are difficult to beat. The most highly scented kinds include delicate Roman hyacinths and multi-flora hyacinths. Their scent is very strong and quite delicious whereas that of the more common large-headed hyacinth varieties have a scent that can turn almost overpowering beyond a certain stage of their life. Multi-flora hyacinth bulbs produce several stems of flowers so they have none of the stiff, top-heavy look of the ordinary varieties. The flowers on each stem of Roman hyacinths are more spread-out and lighter in appearance, rather like a wild hyacinth or English bluebell, and are therefore very graceful and natural-looking.

The tradition of growing hyacinths in pots or glasses dates back to the seventeenth century when, as one of the popular florist flowers of the day, bulbs changed hands for fabulous amounts of money. The hyacinth, which originally came from the Ottoman Empire, was bred and improved from a slender wild flower into the version that we know today. Then as now, single bulbs were often grown in a long, tapering glass specially shaped to hold the bulb just above water. The roots found their way down into the water and became part of the whole effect. Modern versions of the hyacinth glass have become fashionable again so it is easy to find new ones and it is still possible to buy antique flower glasses, often in lovely, rich colours. Children love to plant a bulb and watch it grow and develop. Planted in water in this way it gives them a valuable lesson in how a plant works as well as a sense of achievement when it finally flowers in a spectacular fashion.

Narcissi

Most of the narcissus family – widely known as daffodils – have scent to a greater or lesser degree but the short-cupped Tazetta types have the most powerful fragrance. These varieties come from the Mediterranean region where they grow wild from the Pyrenees to Greece. Unlike trumpet daffodils their small cup flowers are grouped in a bunch on the stem. The well-known varieties 'Cheerfulness' and 'Soleil d'Or' are both sold as cut flowers and often grown as flowering bulbs for the garden or indoors. Their scent can be almost overpowering in a small room but they make easy pot plants and are incredibly welcome early in the year when there is little else in bloom. They are grown commercially in the milder areas of Britain and in the Channel Islands as a cut flower and are some of the first blooms to appear in flower shops, giving a hope of spring. They last well as a cut flower in the house and always seem to look best when they are arranged simply in jugs or plain vases without lots of extra, fussy foliage.

The other group of highly scented narcissus is the poet's narcissus *Narcissus poeticus*. These have a distinctive large perianth of white with a red-ringed eye of yellow stamens that gives them their common name of pheasant's eye. They are the latest narcissi to flower and are best naturalized in grass and wild parts of the garden. *Narcissus poeticus recurvus actaea* is probably the best-known variety. Although it cannot be forced to flower from a bulb indoors it lasts well as a cut flower for arrangements. There is also a double version, which looks a bit like a gardenia, and if you have space anywhere in the garden some of these narcissi should be grown as their scent is very special indeed. The leaves are finer and more grass-like than those of the trumpet daffodils and the flower stems grow to around 60 centimetres (2 feet) in height.

Some of the small species of narcissi have wonderful fragrance and are well worth growing either in troughs and small beds outdoors or

Right. *There are usually sufficient daffodils growing in the garden to allow a small bunch to be picked. They generally have more impact arranged alone without foliage or other materials.*

Below. *A big bowlful of spring flowers on a carpet of bluebells containing scented narcissi, iris, ranunculus and many other blooms.*

as pot plants in a cold greenhouse. *Narcissus canaliculatus* from Sicily is a Tazetta miniature with a very sweet scent. *Narcissus cernuus*, also known as *N. moschatus* because of its musky fragrance, can be grown outdoors in damper, shadier conditions than most narcissi. *N. jonquilla flore pleno*, a taller double form also known as Queen Anne's jonquil, has an intoxicating orangey perfume. Like all the varieties in the jonquil division, it has four to six cup-shaped flowers on each stem. Many of the new hybrids bred from *N. jonquilla* have any number of flowers, varying from two to six. A catalogue from a good nursery that supplies bulbs will offer many different varieties of scented narcissi to grow, some of which are best cultivated in small containers outdoors and others that can be forced in pots and brought into the house.

Crocuses look natural and at their best grown in grass as a colourful carpet. The grass provides some green around them to set off their simple shapes and to augment their skinny foliage.

Crocuses

Generally thought of as a garden flower crocuses are rarely picked and brought indoors, though they are sometimes grown in pebbles or compost in small pots to bloom in the house. Several kinds of crocus, especially the species, are very sweet-scented and seem to be happier grown in pots than the larger-flowered Dutch crocuses that bloom later in the year. Species crocuses can be in bloom in the garden from January onwards, though often the long periods of bad weather without sun at this time of year mean that they never really come into their own and open up their petals to release their scent. When the flowers do open to reveal pollen-filled stamens, insects are quickly attracted and these crocuses provide some of the best early foraging for bees that are on the wing when the sun shines.

Pots planted with bulbs for indoor flowering need a dormant period of dark and cool conditions just as they would have if they were outdoors. Put them in an outbuilding, cellar or cupboard until the shoots appear. They should then be brought into light but not warm conditions until the flowers are on the point of opening. Bringing them into warmth too soon results in tall, stretched stems and feeble flowers. If you have space and the right conditions it is often best to leave pots outdoors until the point of flowering and bring them in for their grand finale. Small pots of species crocus look pretty on a windowsill where they will catch plenty of light to open up their flowers, and stood on low tables where you can really appreciate their pretty, often striped petals and golden stamens.

E.A. Bowles, who gardened in the early twentieth century at Middleton House in London, was an expert on bulbs and bred many new varieties of early crocus from *Crocus chrysanthus*. Many of these were highly scented even though the original parents were not.

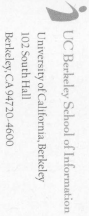

UC Berkeley School of Information

University of California, Berkeley
102 South Hall
Berkeley, CA 94720-4600

fiat lux

Mrs. Alida Wilson
212 Knight Dr
San Rafael CA 94901-1430

551-37-5040

'Snow Bunting' has creamy-white flowers deepening to yellow in the centre with an orange stigma and a faint bluish-mauve feathering on the back of the petals. It has a strong scent, which is particularly noticeable indoors. 'Princess Beatrix' is another good choice with its clear mauvey-blue coloration, while 'Cream Beauty' is a rich, buttery cream colour with a brownish-mauve reverse to the petals. As all of these varieties are quite small and delicate they are best planted outdoors in places where they will not be smothered or overgrown by larger plants: among alpines, at the front of borders, in troughs, tubs and window-boxes. Some species such as *Crocus thomasinianus* are perfect for naturalizing in short grass where they rapidly seed themselves and spread into a large mauve carpet after a few years. Bear this in mind before planting this variety in a border where the seedlings might not be so welcome.

SCENTED HOUSE-PLANTS

During the long months of early spring when there are few fresh flowers in the garden and no great choice in the flower shops either, scented house-plants come into their own. They provide a focus to a room and some give a much needed boost of colour too at this dreary time of the year. Indoor flowering plants that charm us from a shop window or market stall are often bought on a whim to cheer us up on a cold, grey day.

Jasmines

Many types of flowering house-plant have a short life, even with the best treatment, but one outstanding plant, which seems happy no matter what, is *Jasminum officinale*. Outdoors this small-leaved, evergreen climber will reach up to 3.5 metres (11 feet). Grown in a pot it can easily be contained and trained into all kinds of shapes and still smother itself every year with clouds of small, starry, white flowers with the heady scent unique to jasmine. A jasmine bought as a house-plant in early spring is usually on the point of flowering while garden-grown ones flower later, from around June until October. Indoors or in a greenhouse jasmines often have repeat flushes of flowers throughout the year but even if it is only one magnificent display it is always a joy. *Jasminum officinale* grows wild from Iran across northern India to China. Although it is a common plant it has always been highly prized as a scented flower. The essential oil from jasmine is an important perfume ingredient but is notoriously difficult to extract or to imitate. The associated variety *J. officinale* 'Grandiflorum' has been grown in quantity around Grasse in southern France for centuries. Its oil is extracted by enfleurage, a way of obtaining the scent by layering fat with the flowers (see page 17). Another jasmine closely related to *J. officinale* is *J. polyanthum*. It has white flowers flushed with pink on their back and can only be

These elegant jasmine plants have been trained into various shapes including tall-stemmed standards and simple, narrow pyramids. As wayward stems appear they are quickly twisted between others or tied into place.

grown outdoors in very mild localities but is ideal for conservatories. *J. × stephanense*, which has pink flowers and is hardy outdoors, is another relative.

Standards, hoops and hearts

In time the stems of jasmine will grow quite woody. This can be exploited to turn a small, bushy plant into a tall, elegant standard. Select one strong stem coming from the base of the plant and ruthlessly remove any others. Trim off any branches from the lower half of this stem. Keep the plant growing well and continue to remove anything that interferes with the new stem. Stake the stem against a cane to encourage it to grow straight as to begin with it will be too

Small potted citrus plants need regular liquid feeding. It is important to use an acidic soil suitable for ericaceous plants and to water with soft rainwater if possible.

floppy to hold the weight of leaves and flowers. You will probably need a cane even when your standard is well-established as the stem will never become stiff enough to be self-supporting, although it will turn woody eventually.

A pair of these standards would look good beside an entrance, inside a porch or on either side of a fireplace, for example. Choose good, heavy pots in which to plant them. Keep them in check by weaving and tying in all the wayward shoots, if necessary, to arrive finally at a roughly rounded mop-head effect. It will never be neat like a clipped plant but the general look is natural and pleasing.

Jasmines can be trained into all kinds of other shapes. If they are grown in a pot they will have to be organized into some sort of shape, as they are vigorous, quick growers. You can use canes and sticks or wire to make a framework, twisting new shoots around them and tying or wiring in where necessary. There is no limit to the shapes you can come up with from balls and hearts to pyramids and hoops. The choice will depend on where the plant will eventually stand and what pleases you most. You can be quite tough about pruning out too much growth as jasmines seem to be very good-natured and easy-going plants. If you have space stand them outdoors during the summer months to ripen the wood and induce good flowering the following season. Keep them moist and feed with a regular dose of a liquid general fertilizer.

Citus scents

Plants in the citrus family have a wonderfully useful habit of providing glossy foliage, waxy, white, highly scented flowers and mature and immature fruits all at the same time and for a good part of the year. This means that they hardly ever have an 'off' period, though they really come into their own in the winter and early spring when the fruits ripen and the new flowers begin to bloom. During the summer months keep them outdoors, unless you have perfect greenhouse conditions, as they relish daylight, warmth and rain.

There has recently been a revival of interest in the whole citrus family as indoor plants and many new hybrids have appeared. Miniature oranges and kumquats have replaced orange trees, which with their full-size fruits are not as suitable to keep as a small-scale indoor plant. The genus that includes oranges, lemons and grapefruit originally came from China and Japan. It reached the Mediterranean region early in history, where it has long been grown in Spain, Italy and North Africa. Northern parts of Europe and of the USA can only hope for a good crop of fruit under glass but for centuries these plants have been grown under shelter during the winter and brought out for the summer months. Classic terracotta pots and special tubs were invented that could be transported easily by means of poles pushed through inset loops. In this way many pots were moved outside from their specially built orangeries every season.

The whole citrus plant is scented, from the leaves to the flowers

and fruits. The blossom of the bitter orange *Citrus bigarradia* produces the valuable essential oil known as neroli. These days it is
fabulously expensive but it is still an important component of many
good perfumes and a key ingredient for true eau-de-Cologne.
Neroli oil comes from the flowers while the oil called petit-grain
comes from the leaves, and oil of biggarade from the rind of the fruit.

Children enjoy planting the pips of citrus fruits and watching
them grow into little plants on a windowsill. Although the tiny trees
are unlikely to produce viable fruit, it is still fun to do. Plant the pips
in seed compost in small plastic pots or old yoghurt cartons and
label and date them. Keep them damp but never too wet until the
small, green shoots appear. Some pips never germinate but the suc-
cess rate is generally quite high. There are some varieties that have
been bred specially for pot culture. These include *Citrus limon*
'Meyer's Lemon', one of the hardiest varieties. *Citrus taitensis*, or
Otaheite orange, makes a small, bushy plant ideal as a pot plant with
particularly scented flowers. Small, decorative oranges are produced
in abundance and are at their best at the end of the year. *C. medica*
produces large, narrow citron fruits that are used for candying. It
has very large, fragrant flowers with purple undersides.

All citrus plants are best watered with soft rainwater. They can
sometimes become infested with aphids or scale insects, both of
which lead to sticky, sooty leaves. Keep a watch out for either insect
and respond quickly if they appear. Scale insects can be particularly
difficult to get rid of once they have a hold. A systemic insecticide,
which gets into the sap and kills any insect that tries to feed from it,
is usually the most effective means of eradication.

Preserving peel

Dried lemon- and orange-peel is a useful ingredient to have for
culinary and scenting purposes and extremely easy to prepare. Use
your own home-grown citrus fruits if possible or try to buy un-
sprayed, unwaxed fruits. With a small, very sharp knife pare away
the peel, taking care not to include much white pith. Hang the coils
of peel above a regular heat source, such as a solid-fuel cooker, or
spread them out on a rack or basket in a warm linen-cupboard.
When they are dry they can be used whole or ground into a powder
in a small electric grinder. If you want small pieces of whole peel for
pot-pourri or scented bags it is easier to cut it when fresh rather than
trying to cut the hard, dried peel into tiny shreds or squares. Store
the prepared peels in air-tight jars until you want to use them. A
pinch of ground orange-peel is delicious in casseroles or soups and
in puddings, cakes and biscuits. The dried coils of lemon turn a pale
and pretty yellow and look lovely piled into a shallow bowl, either
alone or partnering another scented material such as eucalyptus
leaves or whole spices. The colour looks excellent when contrasted
with dried lavender and adds texture and bulk to citrussy pot-
pourris based on lemon verbena and other lemon-scented leaves.

Cut citrus peels into tiny squares before you dry them as it is far easier to do this while the peel is soft and fresh. Keep some strips in long, complete coils for decorative purposes.

CITRUS SKIN TONIC

The long, cold winter months often leave skin looking and feeling dull. This slightly astringent skin tonic is easy to make and guaranteed to enliven the complexion.

INGREDIENTS

8 tablespoons orange flower
   water
2 tablespoons chopped lemon-
   peel
2 tablespoons chopped orange-
   peel

1 tablespoon freshly squeezed
   lemon juice
1 cardamom pod
6 tablespoons alcohol (vodka
   or eau-de-vie)
½ teaspoon tincture of benzoin

METHOD

Put everything into a large, screw-topped jar and leave to infuse, shaking it each day. After a week strain the liquid through double muslin or a coffee filter into a clean bottle.

SOWING SCENTED ANNUALS FOR SUMMER

Spring is a busy season in the garden. Gardeners often have to juggle time spent dealing with maintenance jobs at the end of another winter and getting ahead and doing all the special extras for the new season. If you are to have a display of scented annuals such as sweet peas and nicotiana later in the summer, now is the time for sowing seeds then pricking out the small seedlings after germination.

You may simply prefer to buy small plants nearer the time, but by growing your own you can choose distinctive colours and varieties and not boxes of mixed types. Like many of the annuals that can be grown to edge borders or fill tubs sweet peas can be sown straight into the ground once the soil has warmed up a little. By planting them in pots under cover, however, you can bring their flowering forward a little and give them a good start during the time when weather can be cold and unpredictable and cruel to young plants, even the hardy sweet pea. Some people sow sweet peas in autumn and let them overwinter as small plants for very early blooms, particularly if they are exhibiting them at shows, but early spring is usually the best time for the average gardener to sow them.

The choice of sweet-pea varieties is overwhelming. There are single-coloured types as well as good old mixtures of colours and special ones bred for exhibiting. If fragrance is your first criterion then look for mixtures of seed sold as old-fashioned sweet peas. Smaller, simpler flowers are compensated for by an interesting range of unusual colours and a powerful, true sweet-pea scent. The old-fashioned kinds have solid pastel shades, which are less aggressive than the transparent, screaming colours of the newer kinds.

The breeding of the sweet pea into the flower we know today is a fairly recent happening. The simpler, plainer types were quickly developed into frilled-edged blooms with several blossoms on each long, straight stem. The sweet pea *Lathyrus odoratus* is the scented only member of the genus. Other types have quite small, pretty flowers and a wide colour range, but no scent.

The small, round seeds of sweet peas are immensely hard. Some gardeners carefully chip a tiny sliver of outer-seed coating off the pea to help germination. This is fiddly and not really necessary. Be careful not to overwater the newly sown seeds in the belief that it will soften them up as they can sometimes rot in the soil if they are too wet. Plant in single, small pots or a seed tray. Single pots are a sensible choice as the long roots can get away into growth well and they are not disturbed too much at planting-out time. One problem, however, is that lots of small pots take up a great deal of room on a windowsill or greenhouse bench.

Germination takes about ten to twenty days at a temperature of 12° to 13° C (55° to 56° F) but seeds can be given more heat than this to speed things up. Once you have small plants they should have their tops picked off to encourage strong growth from their base. If you are aiming for especially large flowers on long, straight stems you may want to grow them as cordons by careful training of the plant up a single stem. If you simply want a mass of blooms and scent in the garden and lots of flowers to pick then plant them to scramble up a structure of hazel twigs, canes or netting.

Planting Scented Lilies

Another job for early spring is to plant scented lilies in tubs and flower borders. While many lily varieties have spectacular flowers, only certain types have lovely scents.

The Asiatic hybrids with large, outward-facing flowers are the type most commonly grown as florists' cut flowers, but they have little or no scent. Look for certain types from the Oriental hybrid group and many of the species. 'Casablanca' is a pure-white, late-flowering *auratum* lily with an outstanding fragrance. 'Imperial Silver' and 'Imperial Gold' with freckles on a white base smell delicious too. 'Stargazer' has deep crimson-pink flowers with paler edges and a powerful scent and is happy grown in pots or a border. *Lilium auratum* from Japan, the parent of many of the newer hybrids, has white flowers with yellow bands down the inside of the

Above. *Small nicotiana plants are ready to be separated and planted-out with more room between them, while another batch of tiny seedlings from the propagator is inspected for progress.*

Left. *Sweet peas have large, round seeds that are easy to handle and can be sown individually unlike the tiny seeds of many annuals.*

Lily bulbs can be planted singly in pots or grouped together. As they produce several flowers on a stem one plant in a pot does not look lost or meagre. Bulbs showing signs of top-growth are fresh and alive but must be handled carefully.

petals and crimson spots all over them.

Most people know *Lilium candidum* as the Madonna lily and it was once a common sight in jumbled cottage gardens. It is much rarer now and one of those plants difficult to get established. The lily of medieval paintings, it was grown then and for centuries afterwards as a church decoration. The scent is very beautiful and rather like heather honey. It is one of the few lilies to thrive in alkaline soils though it is not suitable for pot culture. The flowers are pure white.

The *Lilium regale* plant has a faint purplish tinge to the backs of the trumpet-shaped flowers. One of the best and easiest lilies to grow in the garden or in pots, the regal lily is good-natured and unfussy. On a warm, still summer evening the golden-centred flowers will scent the whole garden with a honeysuckle perfume. If you are growing lilies for the first time, start with this species. There is also a prolific, pure-white version, *Lilium regale album. Lilium longiflorum* is another white-flowered scented species with very long, slender trumpets. It is often sold as a cut flower and sometimes called the Easter lily. Its scent is similar to jasmine. It is very amenable as a pot-grown plant and can be forced into early flowering but is not suitable for planting into borders in most gardens.

The two *martagon* lilies, white and purple, have little turk's-cap flowers, which are slightly scented at night, attracting hawk-moths for pollination. From Nepal where it grows on grassy hillsides is *Lilium wallichianum*, which produces enormous flowers on a stem 1.2 to 1.5 metres (4 to 5 feet) tall. The flowers are long, narrow trumpets, greenish white and highly scented. They come into bloom in late summer.

Pots and bulbs

Most lilies need to be planted fairly deep so pots must be tall and generous. Bulbs can be planted singly or in groups of three, five, seven or whatever you have room for, as odd numbers always look best. The pot material will depend on budget, aesthetics and personal preference but choose something heavy as some lilies get very tall and need a secure, sturdy base. A soil-based compost is the best choice of growing medium as it will provide support and not dry out as fast as soil-less mixtures do. All lilies like good drainage so spend time making a good layer of gravel or crocks at the bottom of the pot and lighten the soil with a little sharp sand or horticultural grit. Make sure the bulbs are not touching each other, spacing them 3 to 4 centimetres (1½ inch) apart, and cover them with soil. Leave them until the shoots appear and then keep them in an open but sheltered place and water regularly. Feed with liquid fertilizer once they have begun flowering and continue to do so after the flower stem has been cut down as it is important that the plant rebuilds strength through its stems and leaves for the following year. Shorter-growing varieties will not need staking but most lilies need some support as their enormous flowers on quite thin stems make them very top-heavy. Use canes pushed in carefully to avoid the bulbs or a network of bushy twigs. The lower parts of lily plants are never very attractive so a support does not detract much from the whole plant.

A SPRING POT-POURRI

The spring does not seem an obvious season for making pot-pourri. Many of the traditional recipes and mixtures are based on a lavish use of heavily scented rose petals and summer flowers, which are abundant later in the year. But the early-flowering bulbs and other spring blooms should not be overlooked as valuable material for making some of the prettiest pot-pourri mixtures.

Without the use of rose petals it can be slightly more difficult to find enough strongly scented flowers during spring. The way to get around this is to use extra ingredients, such as citrus peel and perhaps lemon-scented leaves, to add any zest that may be lacking. One big advantage of spring flowers is their vivid colour, which remains even after drying, and the strong shapes and lovely petal textures of flowers such as daffodils and tulips.

Spring scents are generally quite light and fresh compared with the richer, heavier scents of summer flowers but this simply makes

A marvellous collection of spring flowers, many of which can be dried for use in a pot-pourri. Tulips and ranunculus keep their strong colours very well.

for a delicious change from all the rose-based pot-pourris that can be made later in the year. Even if you do not want to make a spring mixture it is a good idea to collect and dry spring flowers as they appear and keep them stored for use in general pot-pourris later in the year.

You can use all kinds of garden flowers or flowers from a florist's arrangement that are past their best. If you prepare small batches at a time you will quickly build up an excellent store of ingredients. Freesias, for example, dry really well, retaining their colour and scent and make a good base for a spring pot-pourri. Only one or two kinds of tulips, such as *Tulipa sylvestris*, are scented. They all dry well, however, and are quite bulky, which is useful as so many

Prepare individual flowers for drying by removing stems and unwanted leaves and spreading the heads or large petals out on a wire rack or muslin-covered tray. Dry over a suitable, gentle heat-source, turning large flowers occasionally.

spring flowers are very small. Daffodils and narcissi work beautifully and are good, inexpensive base ingredients. Other good spring flowers to dry are forsythia, primroses and primulas, auriculas, ranunculus, violets and winter jasmine blossom.

The simplest way to dry small quantities of petals or flower-heads is to lay them on a wire mesh tray or in a basket or colander with plenty of space between blooms and put in a warm place. Ideal drying places can be found at the back of a kitchen range that is permanently warm, or in an airing-cupboard. You should aim to dry them as quickly but gently as possible to keep the colour bright and the scent true. Use a very cool oven as a last resort, but there is a risk of overheating and spoiling the flowers. A bunch of material, such as freesias, can be hung up to dry in a warm place where air circulates freely. However you choose to dry the material, remember that the enemy of dried flowers is damp and humid air.

Once all the flowers are dried, use them either straight away in a spring pot-pourri or store them in their individual varieties or colours in air-tight bags, tins or glass jars. Keep stored flowers out of the light so that they keep their colour as long as possible.

A SPRING POT-POURRI RECIPE

This recipe is inspired by all the golden yellows that are abundant at this time of year. The scent is fresh, light and lemony, but most of all this is a pot-pourri for visual effect. A bowl of this mixture placed in any situation creates its own patch of sunlight on dull, cold days. The ingredients have been worked out proportionally rather than by weight. Use an average-sized teacup for measuring, though it is not too important that quantities are exact. After you have made one or two recipes you will find that you start to invent or adapt recipes to suit your own particular taste.

The finished spring pot-pourri is bold and bright with lots of texture and large flower heads to give visual interest. Display in a large, shallow container to show it off best.

INGREDIENTS

3 cups dried daffodil heads
3 cups dried yellow tulip heads
1 cup dried yellow ranunculus heads
1 cup mixed small yellow dried flower-heads e.g. primroses

Dried peel of one orange and one lemon
5 cinnamon sticks
½ cup orris root powder
8 drops lemon verbena or lemon balm essential oil

METHOD

In a large bowl mix all the flowers together by hand. Add the dried peels torn into fairly small pieces and the cinnamon sticks broken into short lengths. Add the orris root powder and combine everything well. Finally add the drops of essential oil and stir well to distribute it throughout the mixture. Put the mixture into large paper bags and fold over the tops, securing them with paper clips or a clothes peg. Leave the bags of pot-pourri in a dry, warm and dark place for about six weeks to cure. Every few days take out the bags and give them a vigorous shake. When the pot-pourri has cured put into a container and decorate the top with extra dried flowers or whole blooms. One large golden lily flower-head dried in a desiccant would look lovely sitting on the top of this spring pot-pourri.

SCENTED FRESH-FLOWER ARRANGEMENTS AND POSIES

At this time of year flower scents are mostly fresh and invigorating and sometimes quite subtle. All the small wild flowers of the season, such as primroses, cowslips and violets, have distinctive scents but they are not generally strong enough to carry on the air. Small posies are one of the best ways of capturing the spring scents of the garden and they are traditionally given as presents at this time of the year.

As there is not a large range of flowers to choose from yet, use one highly scented flower and mix it with other non-scented material plus small, scented herbs and foliage. Some of the winter-flowering shrubs may still be in bloom, such as mahonia and shrubby honeysuckles and possible some of the daphnes and *Viburnum × bodnantense*. As spring progresses the small, white flowers of the shrub *Osmanthus delavayi* should be perfuming the whole garden. Little sprays of this shrub are lovely used in indoor arrangements and posies. It has small, pointed, glossy green leaves on stiff, straight stems, which set off the tiny, tubular, strongly scented flowers. Sprigs of evergreen myrtle are good to add to posies. Although the shrub is not yet in flower, myrtle leaves have a warm, spicy scent all year round. Many of the early-flowering prunuses have scented flowers. The pretty clusters of blossom, often on bare stems, somehow always suggest that they *should* smell delicious, even if they are unscented. Perhaps pink flowers hint at having a fine scent, though this often not the case.

Choosing flowers for a spring posy is easy if you have primroses, primulas, polyanthus and auriculas. They all have wonderful scents, which are more intense in warm surroundings, so they are lovely to bring indoors. Their colours range from white and cream through the subtlest shades of bronze, green and grey in the auricula family to the bright and cheerful blues, oranges and brilliant yellows of polyanthus and garden primroses. They are tough and hardy and do not even seem to mind endless days of rain on their velvety petals. They are therefore one of the best plants to fill tubs and window-boxes for a spring display of colour.

ANTIQUE AURICULAS

The *Primula auricula* species has a charm and fascination about it that has recently attracted a revival of interest among gardeners and plant enthusiasts. With varietal names like 'Old Red Dusty Miller', 'Old Suffolk Bronze', 'Osborne Green' and 'Blue Velvet' it has an

A softly fragrant posy of spring flowers. Cowslips and primroses combine with the miniature blooms of sky-blue forget-me-nots. This would make a perfect Mother's Day gift or token of affection for anyone who loves simple, wild country flowers. A linen tape as a ribbon adds a little more home-spun charm to the pretty posy.

antique feel to it. Many modern varieties can be traced back to the days when auriculas were shown at competitions held by florists' societies or displayed under cover in elaborate theatres to protect the dusty bloom that covers the leaves and flowers of some types. Auricula theatres were made from wood. They had a stage, rows of shelves and sometimes even a curtain. Aurciulas are descended from *Primula auricula* and *Primula × pubescens*, the scented alpine cousins of the wild cowslip. In the eighteenth century much hybridizing was done and specimens were known to change hands for large sums of money.

Today there are the easy alpine and border types of auricula and the more difficult 'show' or 'stage' plants. They are all hardy but do

not relish very damp conditions, preferring good drainage and a cool, airy situation. The show types are often grown in pots in alpine greenhouses to protect them from wet weather. A display of auriculas in a confined space such as a marquee will scent the air all around with their distinctive fragrance: fresh, slightly fruity and very similar to that of cowslips. It is possible to buy small pots of flowering auriculas in spring from flower shops and nurseries. They can be displayed indoors for the time they are in flower and then planted outdoors when they have finished. Single plants look stylish as they are so theatrical, or you can group several in a larger container such as a basket, mixing colours or staying in one colour range such as dusky purple and mauve or bronze, brown and russet red.

Right. *The strange, velvety petals of auriculas, their stiff stems and neat, organized appearance made them stars of the show-bench in previous centuries. Nowadays we appreciate their subtle colours and delicious cowslip scent and grow them in gardens or containers.*

PLANNING AND PLANTING SUMMER HERBS

The perennial herbs in the garden are all showing some signs of new growth by now except perhaps tarragon, which is much later than most to make an appearance. Annual herbs should be sown early and then at intervals throughout the summer. This will ensure a steady, manageable supply all through the season rather than a glut at one time. If you grow quick crops in the garden, such as lettuce, then think about sowing small rows or patches of dill, coriander, chervil, rocket and purslane as often as you sow the lettuce. Parsley is biennial but it is sensible to sow annually to be sure of a good supply. The herb's notoriously slow germination means that, unless you time it right, it will be too late or too early to transplant your little seedlings. Chives are perennial but can also be sown annually, a sensible option for gardeners who would rather not grow chives in the same spot year after year.

Left. *Parsley plants with different types of leaf – small, curled and plain – are being put into a row between the vegetables in a kitchen garden. Parsley is one of the most useful culinary herbs needed throughout the year. It is a biennial plant but is best replaced every year for fresh supplies.*

You can sow herb seeds in small pots or trays, pricking out plants at the seedling stage and growing them on until big enough to transplant. It is far easier, however, to sow them straight into the ground where they are to grow. Do not be too hasty to sow until the soil has warmed up a bit and is easy to cultivate. Once they have germinated, the small herb plants should be thinned out to give each of them space to develop and then kept watered and free of weeds. Annual herbs, such as dill, are best grown quickly, which means providing them with good soil and lots of moisture. Coriander can quickly run to seed and produce little good leaf if it is starved and left too dry so be sure to give it good soil and to water regularly.

In the sixteenth century, a gluey substance for stiffening ruffs and binding books was extracted from the wild hyacinth, or bluebell. The balsam-like scent carries on the air particularly well when the flowers are growing in a mass. A bluebell-covered beech wood is one of the greatest pleasures of spring.

Perennial herb plants

Certain shrubby herb plants, such as the artemisias, salvias and many other grey- or silver-leaved shrubs benefit from a spring trim. Although they can look ugly through the winter, leaving the leaf gives the plant some protection from extreme cold and frosts, so delay cutting them into shape until at least the middle of spring. Southernwood or lad's love is the common name for *Artemisia abrotanum*, which can be pruned back quite severely as it will shoot into leaf again from just below the cut. The grey-green leaves of southernwood have a curious, pungent, slightly lemony scent, which has the property of keeping away clothes moths and other insects. In France it is known as garde-robe. The culinary sage *Salvia officinalis* or common sage needs to be kept in check and good shape. You can be ruthless with it, cutting the woody stems near to the base of the plant, where they normally shoot again.

Although not strictly a herb, but with scented foliage, catmints (*Nepeta*) are best left alone until the spring rather than being tidied up in autumn. All the perennial herbs that die right back during winter, such as fennel and mint, need no treatment unless you plan to split them up to increase the stock of plants. Clumps of bergamot will begin to show a crop of new shoots along with marjoram and lemon balm. Angelica, a biennial, and sweet cicely, a perennial, both from the large Umbelliferae family are already well into leaf and nearly flowering by mid-spring.

Rosemary is the kind of plant that seems happy to be snipped at and gently pruned throughout the year. This tends to happen naturally as you pick the odd stems for cooking or whatever. The sprawling prostrate kinds, such as *Rosmarinus officinalis prostratus*, need to be gently kept within bounds if they poach another plant's territory. The tall, upright type 'Miss Jessop's Upright' will very slowly form itself into a tall bush over the years and needs little in the way of pruning.

WILD-FLOWER GARDENING

Wild flowers, such as bluebells, primroses, cowslips and violets, are enjoying a revival. More and more gardeners are growing once-common wild species of flowers. This can be quite a difficult thing to do successfully on any scale, particularly in the average small suburban or town garden. If you are lucky enough to have a large country garden, it is possible to create patches or areas of meadow and accompanying plants or a copse or piece of woodland. It is easier to create areas of wild flowers in gardens that resemble their natural habitat rather than starting from scratch. For the majority of gardeners, is probably the most effective strategy to incorporate the successfully translatable types from countryside to garden in among a normal garden setting.

Bluebells

Creating an area of English bluebells (*Hyacinthoides non-scripta*) is a wonderful idea but it will only work properly as a re-creation of a piece of natural country landscape with the right conditions. As with all accompanying woodland plants, bluebells need trees, such as beech, to provide them with slight shade as they begin to bloom. There is no reason, however, why a grassy bank in the shade of a hedge could not be used to grow bluebells. The trick is to be aware of the plant's needs in terms of soil and position and to try to re-create this or find similar conditions in your existing garden. Once established, bluebells can quickly become a nuisance as they seed freely all around them, especially in light, sandy soil conditions. Their scent, though, is one of the real pleasures of spring and they can only be appreciated when they are growing as they do not successfully take to being cut and stood in water indoors.

Primroses

An altogether easier wild-garden flower is the primrose *Primula vulgaris*, which has always been happy tucked in among other plants in country cottage gardens. Given the right conditions of rich soil and special care the garden primrose turns into a plump, well-fed-looking version of its hedgerow cousin. Native to the UK, primroses seed and spread where they are happy and can be planted into borders with other plants or allowed to naturalize in rough grass and under fruit trees or hedges. They thrive in spring sunshine and then cooler, moister conditions for the rest of the year. Their preferred natural habitat is in the damp regions with high rainfall. They can be grown from seed or bought as small plants. It is illegal in the UK to take plants from the wild.

The primrose fragrance is subtle and fresh. Many of the old-fashioned double varieties bred from the original wild primrose lost a lot of their scent along the way. The plain, little, sulphur-yellow 'Prime-role', as it was known as in the sixteenth century, still has the best fragrance.

Cowslips

Primula veris, the cowslip, is from the same family as the primrose. A plant of meadows and grazed land as well as chalk downland, it flowers a little later in the wild. The cowslip has a very special scent likened by some to the sweet breath of a small child. The Saxon vernacular word for the flower was 'cuslippe' as the flower was thought to smell like the breath of a cow. A whole field of cowslips in bloom will scent the air. Generally, however, you need to get close to the tiny, yellow bells hanging in a cluster from the straight, soft, green stem to appreciate the rich but not sickly smell.

Country children were once able to pick bunches of cowslips to

Pale-green stems as soft as chamois leather and the thick, crinkled leaves add even more to the scented charms of a once-common wild flower. The cowslip is a rare treasure these days but easy to establish in a suitable garden.

make into cowslip balls – dense spheres of the flowers, which were used as part of the May-time celebrations. Nowadays the cowslip has been forced to retreat to a very few fields and hedgerows where artificial fertilizers and herbicides have not reached it. Given the right conditions, though, it quickly establishes a small colony and, like the primrose, it can be grown as a border flower or naturalized amongst grass as in the wild. Seed sown one spring will produce plants that will flower by the following year. It is now possible to buy good-sized pot-grown plants in nurseries ready to plant out at any time of the year.

Cowslips were the ingredient for a country wine popular throughout England from medieval times to the nineteenth century. Gallons of little flowers or 'pecks' were needed to make this drink (which shows how common the cowslip once was). Cowslips were candied too, as were primroses, and the blooms were pickled and made into sweetmeats and preserves for the winter months. Old recipes describe primrose tarts and puddings and sweet syrups mostly not to our taste today. Primroses are lovely scattered in a green spring salad or brushed with gum arabic water then dipped in caster sugar to dry crisp and sparkling as a cake decoration.

Violets

The tiny, purple wild violet, hidden away under the shade of its own leaves and growing in woods and on the banks of hedges, has been a favourite flower for centuries. Its elusive scent and its medicinal properties have made it at various times an important plant and through history it has had periods of particular popularity.

In ancient Greece the sweet violet (*Viola odorata*) became the symbol of the city of Athens. In medieval England it held an important role in the kitchen, providing sweetness and fragrance to all kinds of sweet and savoury dishes. The sweet violet has been grown commercially from the very earliest times and much of the crop used in the perfume industry was and still is grown in France. The little dog violet, found growing wild in woods, has no scent so the main garden varieties were bred from *V. odorata*, which is native across northern and southern Europe and to northern Asia; and the Russian violet *V. suavis*, later to flower than *V. odorata*. Double violets have been bred as well as the more common single types. The less-hardy Parma violets, beloved of the Victorians and Edwardians, are strange-looking little flowers, fully double and in several colours, with the most wonderful violet scent.

The violet was always seen as a love potion and serious medicine for diseases of the heart. The tiny bi-coloured field pansy is known as heartsease. This connection may have been more to do with the heart shape of the leaves rather than any real curative powers but violets were used to revive the spirits by being rubbed on the temples and an infusion of the flowers was thought to help sleeplessness.

The scent of violets has been used for perfumes, soaps, lotions and toilet waters. It is still popular today, holding its own among even fashionable, strident, synthetic perfumes. Many people think of the scent of violets as particularly old-fashioned and traditional. It often calls to mind grandmothers or aged great aunts who dabbed handkerchiefs with violet water and were fond of wearing that special shade of grey-mauve known as Parma violet.

The Parma violet is thought to have come from the Orient though its origins are obscure. In its heyday many varieties were available but now it is generally possible to find only three named types: 'Marie Louise', 'Duchesse de Parme' and 'Swanley White' ('Comte Brazzi'). Varieties of other violets are more common and they range in colour from white, pale grey, rose pink and cerise through to the deep purple of the original type. Like primroses they need cool, moist root conditions and must not dry out in summer. They love winter sun and summer shade and can be tucked in among other plants near the front of a mixed border or grown in smaller, more specialized beds. Some varieties, such as 'Coeur d'Alsace', produce large clumps of fairly big leaves after the flowers have finished so they are not the tiny plants that many people expect them to be.

Old books give recipes for violets in salads, syrups and tisanes. There is a liqueur flavoured with violets still available today called, rather over-romantically, Parfait d'Amour. It is an extraordinary deep-purple colour and looks dangerously exotic. It tastes like the little, old-fashioned violet-scented cachous sold to sweeten the breath. Violet vinegar was popular once and jams, jellies and pickles were made with the flowers. People must have grown quite enormous numbers of plants to provide enough of the tiny blooms to indulge in such recipes. Gardening instructions for growing good violets were elaborate and specific. In Victorian times, recipes abounded for violet fertilizer using mixtures such as soot, leaf mould and seaweed. Violets were often cosseted in the luxurious confines of a cold frame to protect them and induce earlier blooming.

The best way to use the scented flowers these days is to make tiny posies and arrangements to enjoy indoors and to scatter the fresh flowers in leafy salads or use them to decorate puddings. The deep-purple flowers look especially pretty on any kind of chocolate cake or dessert dish.

The small bunches of violets sold today, tied with thin cotton and framed with a green ruff of their own heart-shaped leaves or sprigs of ivy, still look like the posies offered from the baskets of Victorian flower-sellers. Disappointingly, however, they are often unscented. This seems to spoil the whole point of a tiny bunch or nosegay.

Violet recipes

Violets are versatile, as the following recipes show, but remember to make them only if you have the flowers growing in your garden. Never pick them from the wild as they are scarce.

An arrangement of tiny violets has to be thought of in miniature. Display the flowers in a thimble or very small glass or jar to create the right scale. Stand the display where it will not get lost among lots of other things. A bedside table might be a good location.

VIOLET TEA

This is the kind of tea, or tisane, that definitely tastes best drunk from thin, china cups rather than large, roomy mugs.

METHOD

Put two tablespoons of fresh violet leaves and one tablespoon of violet flowers into a china jug. Pour over ½ litre (1 pint) of boiling water and leave to infuse for several minutes before serving. You can sweeten it slightly by adding a little honey.

SWEET VIOLET OR COWSLIP WATER

To make the infusion, follow the method in the previous recipe (page 45).

METHOD

Make an infusion with 2 tablespoons of fresh flower heads to 300 millilitres (½ pint) boiling spring water. Leave until cold then strain and add a dash of cider vinegar. It will keep for a day or two but is best used fresh. Use after washing or cleansing the skin by patting the face with cotton wool soaked in the lotion.

VIOLET MILK LOTION

Violets have a gently cleansing effect on the skin and help to keep it clear of blemishes.

METHOD

Gently heat 300 millilitres (½ pint) skimmed milk in a pan until warm. Add 4 tablespoons fresh, sweet violet-heads. Heat gently for about 10 minutes but do not allow the milk to boil. Remove heat and leave to cool. Strain the milk and put it into a bottle. Keep it in the fridge and use as a cleanser. It will keep for only a few days.

CRYSTALLIZED VIOLETS

Along with rose petals, violets are one of the few flowers still crystallized and sold in shops for cake and pudding decoration. This is easy, if a bit fiddly, to do yourself.

METHOD

Dissolve 2 teaspoons of powdered gum arabic in 3 teaspoons of rose-water. Put the solution into a small, screw-top jar and leave for about 3 days, shaking it occasionally. Add more rose-water if necessary to get a thinnish, sticky liquid. With a small, soft paintbrush, spread the paste all over the surface of fresh, dry violets. Leave to dry and harden on a wire rack in a warm place. When crisp and totally dry, use as an edible decoration for cakes and puddings. Store surplus in an airtight container and they will keep for months.

THE SCENTED SPRING GARDEN

As the spring progresses the garden becomes more colourful and flower-filled. Most of the plants that remain dormant over the winter reappear with plenty of fresh, green growth. Flowering shrubs and trees follow one after the other in a succession of bloom. If the weather is cold and unseasonal, some plants are in bloom for a long time; but in other years there can be an unseasonal heatwave and flowers come and go before you really notice them. Everyone hopes for mild, kind weather in which to enjoy the late-spring garden. The colour range of spring plants is still very much dominated

Violets are unusual in that they take up water through their flowers and leaves. Wilting violets will revive if they are completely submerged under water for a while. A less dramatic remedy is to spray the bunch with a fine mist of cool water.

by whites, yellows and blues, but strong accents of colour come from some of the tulips, wallflowers, primulas and polyanthus. A softer colour scheme is provided by pale-pink and white tree blossom and many of the spring-flowering shrubs.

The scents of certain plants at this time of year can be very strong. The waxy-flowered clusters of *Viburnum carlesii* produce an exceptionally sweet, honeyed fragrance that carries in the air as does the scent of the deciduous hybrid azaleas of the Knap Hill types. Wallflowers are a homely, unspectacular kind of plant. They do a useful and often overlooked job, however, of filling the spring borders with a wonderful range of colours and a very special scent.

A cottage garden in late spring is filled with fragrance from the blossom of Viburnum carlcephalum *grown as a small standard, which can be seen in the background. Other spring flowers blooming here are wallflowers, tulips, spring snowflakes, and in the foreground brilliant blue* Omphalodes cappadocica.

47

Wallflowers are mostly from the *Cheiranthus* genus, which is part of the family of four-petalled flowers such as stocks and sweet rocket. The scent of the wallflower is close to that of the pink and carnation and at one time the wallflower was called the wall gillyflower to indicate their similarities.

In the seventeenth century, John Parkinson wrote about the wall-flower: 'the sweetness of the flowers causeth them to be used in nosegays and to deck up houses'. These days, however, they are rarely picked for this purpose and are hardly ever seen for sale as a cut flower. This is a pity because, although they are not the longest-lasting of blooms, they look lovely alone or mixed with other

The heady and exotic fragrance of lily-of-the-valley has been used in perfumes and toiletries for years. The delicate stems of waxy bell flowers, each one wired, were once popular showering down from bridal bouquets.

flowers. The word Cheiranthus means 'handflower', suggesting that wallflowers were once commonly used in posies.

The wallflower is a perennial. Old plants can often be seen flowering high up on walls and stone buildings from seed dropped by birds and, in these conditions, will flower for many years. In gardens, however, we tend to sow or buy wallflowers one year to bloom the following spring and therefore treat them as biennial. To add to the confusion, a few related wallflowers, in the *Erysimum* genus are grown as perennials. Examples are the low-spreading *Erysimum alpinum* with yellow, cinnamon-scented flowers and *Erysimum linifolium* with lilac-coloured flowers.

The wallflower grown as a bedding plant and filler of tubs and window-boxes is *Cheiranthus cheiri*. It comes in seeds of single colours and in mixtures of many colours. If you want a particular, less-common colour, such as a cream or deep-purple, then grow your own plants. Nurseries often offer only the mixtures and there is no way of knowing what colours they will contain until they flower. It is possible to get dwarf, low-growing varieties too, as well as the taller, more straggly wallflower. One especially lovely little wallflower is a variety called 'Harpur Crewe', which has been around for centuries. Double-flowered, deep, golden yellow and very scented, it is always propagated by cuttings and grown as a perennial. The leaves are small and neat and the whole plant is compact and good for a front-of-border position. Known since Elizabethan times, its cheerful colour and rich fragrance make it a perfect plant for the scented spring garden.

Scents for shady places

There is one special spring flower, for which people have always had great affection. Perhaps this is because it has always been used as a flower in wedding bouquets and decorations and has had a symbolic meaning of 'the return of happiness'. Its common name is lily of the valley, once a native woodland plant in northern Europe and parts of the USA, but now a rarity in the wild. It is indeed from the large lily family, though its botanical name is *Convallaria majalis*. This is the only species in the genus and it has distinctive lance-shaped leaves that curl around a spike carrying bell-shaped, waxy white flowers running the length of the stem. Flowering in late spring, lily of the valley thrives in moist, shady places. Its roots slowly spread under the ground, causing the plant to appear in other places. This can be a nuisance in a small garden. It has a strong, spicy, sweet perfume, described in *The Flower Garden* of 1726 as 'the sweetest and most agreeable perfume: not offensive not overbearing, even to those who are made uneasy with the perfumes of other sweet scented flowers'. Perfumes and soaps have been given its scent and the *New Herbal* in 1578 said that the flowers were 'as white as snow and of a pleasant strong savour. The water of the flowers comforteth the heart . . . and doth strengthen the memory'.

The Victorians loved lily of the valley for their posies and magnificently elaborate displays for tables and drawing rooms. They used to dig up roots of the plant while dormant in winter, put them into pots then bring them into warm conditions to force them into bloom. Lily of the valley is still forced to flower early today for the floristry trade. This extends their season, particularly for bridal arrangements. Traditionally, each little stem is finely wired so that it can be bent into graceful shapes showering from the bouquet. If you have a space in the garden, it is lovely to have enough plants so that some flowers can be picked and brought indoors. A border against a north-facing wall is ideal. Although the season is short, the leaves look neat and green for much of the year.

Unexpected scents

Tulips are not considered to have much to offer in the way of fragrance but there are, in fact, several scented varieties.

The delicate, golden-yellow tulip shaded with green at the back of the petals, *Tulipa sylvestris*, is another woodland flower. It has a pronounced scent for a tulip and is one of the few species happy to naturalize in light grass where it increases by means of underground runners. Like many members of the tulip family, though, it likes a good baking of summer sun. Although not commonly seen, *T. sylvestris* is available through many bulb companies and well worth searching out.

Some of the early single tulips are also scented. Within one type the different colours and varieties have a range of scents from lily of the valley and honey to orange blossom. The brilliant-orange flowers of 'De Wet' are sweetly scented, as is a variety called 'Bellona', with rich, gold flowers. The peony-flowered tulip, 'Angelique', has a delicate fragrance and is excellent for picking and using as a cut flower. The flowers are apple-blossom pink and multi-petalled. Two of the exotic, fringed parrot tulips, with their wavy petals and snipped edges, have scent too. The deep-purple almost black tulip called 'Black Parrot' and the orange-scarlet one called 'Orange Favourite', both have scent. So does one of the species, *schrenkii*, a native of Russia, with scarlet flowers edged in yellow growing on short stems and ideal for raised beds and rock gardens.

Plan next year's plantings for beds, containers and pots using a combination of scented tulips and wallflowers. Late-flowering hyacinths can also be useful to add substance, colour and even more fragrance among the softer effect of wallflowers and the taller accents of the tulips.

The glowing burnt orange of tulip petals against a cool blue background. The few scented varieties have a sweet but usually faint fragrance most noticeable in a small room.

Summer
FULL BLOOM

Summer garden fragrances are rich and linger on the heavy air on calm, sultry days. Night-time scents add an exotic touch after the sun has set. Everywhere there are flowers to gather and herbs to harvest while plant essential oils are at their height and perfume at its strongest.

Sweet peas are generous flowers in many senses. Generous in their variety and colours, in their delicious scent and in the prolific quantities of bloom they can produce through the summer.

It is difficult to define quite when summer takes over from spring. We probably all have different views on the matter. But there is a point when countryside and gardens look full and settled and trees lose the fresh, acid, spring-green translucency of their leaves.

One of the first really fragrant summer flowers is the sweet pea. Depending upon when the young plants were set out you can have flowers to pick from quite early in the season. The first few blooms are often short-stemmed, just as the last of the flowers will be, but the more blooms you pick the more there will be to gather later.

Sweet peas need hardly any special treatment to make them look fabulous. If you simply want to enjoy their scent and colour then fill suitable containers with them and stand them in any room where you will smell the powerful, heady fragrance. There is nothing else quite like it. If, however, your sweet peas are of exhibition quality or you prefer a formal arrangement you might want to display them so that each stem is shown off more clearly. Place an old-fashioned pin holder – a spiked device into which the stems lodge – at the base of a wide, shallow bowl.

Sweet peas remain at their best for only a few days when cut but by then there should be another batch to pick. If possible, cut them from the plant either early in the morning or late in the day when it is cool and the plant is not transpiring too much and the flowers will last longer (this applies to any garden flowers that are picked to use indoors). Arrange sweet peas in water only 5 centimetres (2 inches) deep and use a cut-flower food to extend their life even further.

Many other scented flowers suitable for arrangements can now be picked or bought. The first roses appear and sweet Williams and pinks begin their good, long season. Lilac, philadelphus and stocks all emphasize that summer has arrived and the short peony season ends all too soon. There are many different herbs to pick both for the kitchen and for flower arrangements. Sweet cicely is covered with large, creamy flowers, and sweet woodruff bursts into bloom with hundreds of tiny, clean, white, starry blossoms.

Many of the different irises that bloom at the start of the summer have a variety of scents. None of them are really strong but they have the kind of subtle fragrances that are worth discovering even if it means getting down on your hands and knees to sniff at the flowers. The tall bearded iris is descended from several species including *Iris pallida*, which is strongly perfumed. John Gerard, who wrote his famous *Herball* in 1597, grew it in his garden in Holborn soon after its introduction to England in Elizabethan times. He commented that 'the flowers do smell exceeding sweete, much like the orange flower'. The scent has also been described as being like vanilla or even civet. You can grow the species *I. pallida* or choose one of the many colours of bearded iris, which owe their existence to hybridization with *I. pallida* and other species.

There are also many varieties of iris known as beardless iris, including one very important species, *Iris florentina*. A native of southern Europe, this flower came to be the heraldic emblem of the

A cool mixture of white and mauve sweet peas in a large water jug fills a room with the essence of summer. Sweet peas invariably look good packed densely together in this way.

city of Florence and is thought to be one of the oldest plants in cultivation. We know that it had been introduced into Egypt by 1500 BC. It has one very special property that gave it its important role throughout history. The flowers are not very spectacular or beautiful, though pretty in a subtle way, but the rhizomatous root, when dried, has the perfume of violets. This dried rhizome is the substance known as orris root and an alcoholic extraction of it forms frangipani, one of the most enduring perfumes known. Orris root contains irone, the same chemical present in violets, though the iris version is a compound and not as pure as that of violets. In medieval times pieces of the dried root were placed among stored clothes or burnt to produce a rich perfume to freshen musty rooms. Ground orris root powder is the best and most commonly used fixative of other scents in home-made pot-pourri.

One other species of iris has had a similar use in the past. The rhizome of *Iris pseudacorus*, the wild yellow flag and symbol of medieval France, produces an essential oil with a delicate perfume. It was used as a substitute for the oil from *Acorus calamus*, the sweet rush, a strewing herb in medieval times. This iris needs to

There are several scented varieties of iris, though others have little or no scent. They are short-lived blooms but spectacular while they are in flower.

grow at the edge of water or in very damp, boggy conditions. In the wild it flourishes in deep ditches and by streams, rivers and ponds.

Other scented summer irises include the Spanish iris, which is easy to grow, and the Juno iris, which requires long hours of summer sunshine to thrive and is therefore not always the easiest plant to grow successfully in cooler climates.

SUMMER LEAVES AND HERBS

Many deliciously scented leaves get overlooked and overshadowed by showier scented flowers. During the summer months, however, there are many foliage fragrances worth discovering, either to enjoy fresh or to preserve in some way for later in the year.

Sweet woodruff

A part of a productive herb garden in early summer includes the first startling pink blooms of Rosa gallica officinalis, *the leaf spikes of* Iris florentina, *golden feverfew, sweet cicely, wood strawberries, tiny lemon-yellow violas, lily regale in bud,* Lavandula pedunculata viridis, *and* Origanum rotundifolium.

Sweet woodruff *Asperula odorata* is a low-growing plant with masses of narrow, pointed leaves circling the stem along its whole length and tiny, white, star-shaped flowers. The leaves are the most fragrant part of the plant as they contain the chemical coumarin. They have little or no apparent scent when fresh but while drying and once dried, release a fragrance like new-mown hay. Certain grasses, such as sweet vernal grass, also contain coumarin. Sweet woodruff was a favourite material for medieval garlands that decorated churches on feast days. This was partly because of its scent and partly because any pure-white flower was popular at the time. Much later the Victorians used woodruff in summer claret drinks and, in Europe, it has long been used to flavour wines and mixed drinks.

Grow sweet woodruff as ground cover in a shady part of the garden or herb bed. It is ideal used to cover bare soil at the base of large shrubs or let loose in grass or under wild hedges. Sweet woodruff spreads rapidly and can become a nuisance, weaving its tangle of little, orange roots among other plants. It flowers in the early months of summer. Pick the leaves slightly later for drying and using in pot-pourris or little scented pillows and sachets.

Pick whole stems and spread them on wire mesh or muslin or lay them loosely in shallow baskets. Leave to dry in a sunny greenhouse or indoors in a warm room or airing cupboard. Try to do this as quickly as possible to retain leaf colour and maximum scent. When completely dry, rub the leaves off the stems and store them in tins, jars or boxes until needed.

Another way to use this lovely herb is to do as the Elizabethans once did and make small bunches of fresh woodruff. Hang these high up around a room to release their scent slowly and freshen the air. While the leaves are young and fresh use the following recipe to make a summer wine cup, which will evoke memories of summer garden parties and lawn tennis.

For a refreshing summer drink, infuse a handful of lemon balm Melissa officinalis *in a small amount of boiling water. Leave until cool. Strain, add freshly-squeezed lemon juice and ice, and sweeten to taste. Drink outdoors.*

SUMMER WINE CUP
This makes approximately enough for six to eight people.

INGREDIENTS

1 bottle red wine
1 bottle chilled white wine
1 bottle chilled sparkling white wine

1 wine glass brandy
1 large bunch sweet woodruff
8 sugar cubes

METHOD

Put the sweet woodruff and the sugar cubes into a large bowl and pour over the brandy and half the bottle of red wine. Leave for an hour to macerate. When ready to serve, strain out the woodruff, stir well to dissolve the sugar and add the other wines. Serve with a fresh sprig of woodruff in each glass. You can substitute the sparkling wine with mineral water if you prefer less alcohol.

PINEAPPLES, GINGER AND LEMONS

The *Salvia* genus contains many plants with strongly scented leaves. Most people know the culinary sages but the little-known pineapple sage *Salvia rutilans* produces one of the most delicious scented leaves. It makes a bushy plant with large, rough leaves and crimson flowers, and grows to a height of about 60 centimetres (2 feet). It is probably best grown in a pot or container and taken into a frost-free greenhouse during the winter months. The leaves give off a fruity, pineapple smell when brushed or squeezed, which is quite unlike any other plant.

There is another plant that has the fragrance of pineapples, but this time from the flowers: the tall shrub *Cytisus battandieri*, a native of Morocco. It has lovely yellow, lupin-like flowers, which give out the scent of the ripe fruit. This wonderful plant is best grown against a wall for protection from cold winds. A good position is beside windows or doors that can be left open during the still, warm days of summer so that the fragrance from the flowers can drift inside the house.

The whole genus of mints *Mentha* has what we know as a mint fragrance, yet there are subtle differences. The peppermints and the spearmints, for example, are distinctively different aromatic variations on the minty theme. There are also several mints that have an extra fragrance almost superimposed upon their underlying mintiness. There are green-apple and eau-de-Cologne scents, even one with a hint of ginger to it. Ginger mint is a particularly pretty mint with small leaves splashed with yellow. Like many of the mints its roots need containing if it is not to spread throughout the garden.

Tree Fragrances

Unless they are spectacularly showy, tree blossoms often go unnoticed in the garden and countryside. Some large forest trees, such as lime and beech, have insignificant green flowers that are nevertheless very attractive to honey-bees and other insects. Some of the most deliciously flavoured honeys are made from tree blossoms and they provide valuable forage for insects throughout the spring and summer. The wild hawthorn and the cultivated forms of this tree are in bloom for three weeks or so at the point where spring gives way to summer. The garden forms often have double flowers. These come in deep-pink and red versions as well as the more common creamy-white, but they all have a strong, almondy perfume, which is rich and sweet. The flowers are normally so abundant that the scent carries in the air.

Around mid-summer the flowers of the hedgerow elder tree *Sambucus niger* come into bloom. Their musk-like scent is very powerful, in some kinds verging on the unpleasant, but certainly cannot be ignored. The species *Sambucus canadensis* has the best muscatel fragrance. Many country recipes use its fragrance to flavour drinks and puddings. Traditionally, a head of frothy, white elder flowers was cooked with gooseberry dishes to add a subtle taste of muscat.

The lime or linden tree has fragrant flowers that bees find extremely attractive. Most varieties of lime are too big for normal gardens but there is a small variety with fragrant yellow flowers called *Tilia tomentosa* or silver lime.

There are many trees, too, with scented foliage or even bark. One lovely tree that doesn't grow too large for most gardens and has an elegant, pyramidal growth shape is the balsam poplar. The buds are covered in a sticky resin and, as they unfold in spring, the garden is

filled with their clean, fresh balsam scent. On warm days throughout the summer, the leaves continue to emit this scent. Look for the Tacamahac or balsam poplar *Populus balsamifera*. Another species, *P. candicans*, the Ontario poplar or balm of Gilead, has larger leaves but the same balsam scent.

HAWTHORN-BLOSSOM LIQUEUR

An old-fashioned recipe revived. It is said to taste better than the best cherry brandy.

METHOD

Fill a glass preserving jar with the clean flower heads of hawthorn. Make sure they are loosely packed and that any bits of green leaf or stem have been removed. Take 225 grams (8 ounces) castor sugar to 600 millilitres (1 pint) of brandy and gently warm the brandy with the sugar to dissolve it. Pour it over the flowers to fill the jar then seal the lid tightly and leave the jar in a warm dark place for at least three months to infuse, shaking it occasionally. Strain the brandy through a double thickness of muslin then rebottle and store.

THE SUMMER POT-POURRI

Although it is possible to make pot-pourris all year round, the best and easiest time is during the summer months when there is plenty of every kind of flower and herb at their scented best. Pick and collect material little and often so that through the weeks you gather lots of ingredients that can be combined at a later date when time is not so precious and the weather forces you to be indoors.

If, however, you want to make an old-fashioned moist pot-pourri (see page 62) you will need to start now and add to it slowly as the summer progresses. It 'makes itself' throughout the process and just needs curing at the end. Most modern pot-pourris are based around dried flowers and petals to which scent has been added, though some of the ingredients may be scented to start with. A moist pot-pourri relies on the original ingredients for its scent and, made properly, should retain its scent for many years. The drawback is that it does not look pretty so it is usually kept in a lidded container and opened when needed.

A dry summer pot-pourri

On fine, dry days, pick flowers and leaves and spread them out on wire mesh, trays or shallow baskets. Dry them quickly. You could leave them in the warmth of the sun, but not in direct sunlight or

The finished results of hawthorn-blossom liqueur made early in the summer should be savoured with some style and a sense of occasion.

when the atmosphere is too humid. Alternatively, dry them above a kitchen range or in a warm airing-cupboard. Rose petals are the first and obvious choice but all kinds of flowers are worth experimenting with. Summer jasmine dries well and holds its magnificent scent, though it turns a creamy brown when dried as do most white flowers. Cornflowers and hardy geraniums provide welcome deep-blue and purple colour but add no scent. Many herb leaves dry well and keep their scent. Collect ingredients such as lemon balm, lemon verbena, thyme, rosemary, marjoram, bay leaves, woodruff, savory, artemisia leaves, myrtle and sage.

Dry a few large-scale, whole flower-heads, such as peonies and old-fashioned roses. These can either be pulled apart into separate petals later or used decoratively as complete flowers to add texture and a more dramatic look. Keep various flower types separate if you wish to use them for several different recipes later. If you are making just one summer pot-pourri, however, don't worry about mixing the flowers together right from the start as the process will then take up less space and fewer utensils. When your petals and flowers are dry and ready, sprinkle a little powdered orris root in with them to fix their scent and preserve them until you wish to use them.

A moist summer pot-pourri

A moist pot-pourri is made from a main base of rose petals pickled in salt. It usually has other plant and flower ingredients added to it later, such as jasmine or lavender. To make it successfully you must have a good source of highly scented red or deep-pink garden rose petals in quantity. You do not need them all at the same time so they can be picked in succession through the summer. Florists' roses are

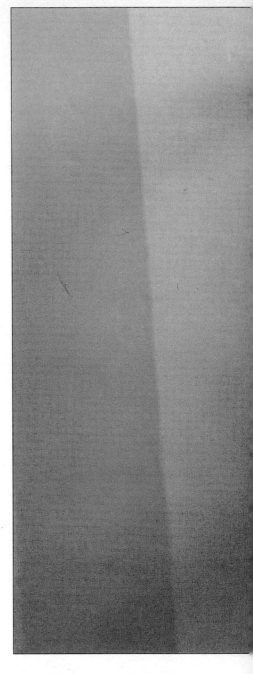

Left. *The enormous, many-layered flower heads of rich, pink peonies are an all-too-short summer garden pleasure. Plant plenty of these flowers so that there are enough to bring indoors where they last well as a cut flower and look simple and elegant arranged alone as shown here.*

Above. Peonies are a useful addition to pot-pourri as they have masses of petals that dry well. Whole heads dried intact make excellent decorations. Hang the stems somewhere warm and they will continue to open out as they dry.

rarely scented enough. Use varieties such as the dark-red climbing rose 'Guinée', any red Gallica roses, 'Souvenir du Dr Jamain' and some modern, deep-red, hybrid tea-roses such as 'Crimson Glory'.

Pull the petals from the rose and, if you have time, take off the little, white crescent at the base of the petal. This can be done quickly with your fingers or more slowly with small scissors. The next important stage is partly to dry the petals until they are leathery. Spread them out in a single layer and leave in a warm place for a few days until they reach this stage. Then put a layer of petals in a large earthenware bowl or wide-necked jar and sprinkle a layer of

A morning's pickings from the garden spread out to dry makes perfect material for a pot-pourri. Roses predominate but many other flowers dry well to add different colours and textures to the final recipe.

coarse, non-iodized salt over the petals. Put a plate or saucer on top and weigh this down with a heavy weight or a stack of full food tins. Leave the mixture in a cool place and give it a good stir every day. When you have enough newly picked petals, make another layer plus salt, and so on throughout the summer. After six weeks or so you should have a brown, crumbly mass. To finish the pot-pourri, add other dried flowers and leaves according to what you have. Lavender, scented geranium leaves, bay leaves, lemon verbena, pot-marigold petals, jasmine, rosemary, lemon balm and mint leaves are all good options.

The next stage is to add a fixative and spices for more fragrance. It is difficult to give hard-and-fast rules for the amounts of ingredients needed as much will depend on how many rose petals you have used. The best and cheapest fixative is ground orris root. Add about 1 tablespoon to 2 mugs of the rose-petal mixture. Stir well and add some ground allspice, cloves, cinnamon, nutmeg, and mace, stirring and sniffing until you have a pleasing result. A few pieces of dried lemon- and orange-peel are a good addition. Finally, a drop or two of essential oil is useful if the fragrance needs boosting. Rose geranium is a good choice. Pure-rose essential oil is very expensive.

Put the pot-pourri into large paper bags and fold over the tops, securing them with a peg or paper clip. Put them away in a cool, dark place for at least six weeks to cure, giving them an occasional shake. Finally, put the mixture into small, lidded jars, closed baskets or special pot-pourri containers.

A ROSE CELEBRATION

The rose is the classic scented flower. Even if it had no scent it would still remain a powerfully symbolic image. Through history it has been a lovers' token, a religious symbol, the emblem of countries and kings, a celebratory decoration and an inspiration to artists and poets. It is the most popular and widely grown garden plant and always a first choice for bouquets and arrangements. Apart from all this, and the endless variety of types and colours the rose comes in, it has one very special quality: its scent.

An ingredient of perfumes, lotions and sweet waters from the earliest times, the scent of roses is complex and varied. While there is one definite, recognizable rose scent, there are many variations. Different types of rose are described as having the scent of raspberries, orange, musk, vanilla, tea, incense, lemon or apricots. Much of the breeding and hybridization of roses that has taken place has ignored the scent in a quest for new colours and forms of flower, though it would be unfair to suggest that all modern roses lack scent.

The enormous rose family is split into groups ranging from the wild species to modern hybrids. Such a vast range often makes choosing roses difficult. For the gardener interested in scent, these problems are compounded by the information supplied about roses, which tends to list the plants' flower colour, style and habit – whether it is a climber or a shrub – often omitting a description of its fragrance. This is because so many gardeners do not regard scent as their first priority. To help remedy this situation, there is a list of roses on pages 154-155 that includes only the best scented types and gives all other necessary information.

Rose recipes

We are great growers of roses but not great users of the flowers. At one time roses were employed abundantly in the kitchen, bathroom

and sickroom. Rose syrups and medicines soothed winter ailments. Rose-water was sprinkled on clothing and over household guests when they arrived after a long journey. Rose-buds were pickled for salads. Rose petals were made into beads and scented sweet powders, and petals were strewn in Roman banqueting halls and showered over new brides. Conserves and jams made from roses were stored away for special occasions, and sweetmeats and crystallized petals were provided at feasts and dinners. Roses flavoured wine and vinegar, syrups and honey. There seemed no end to the uses to which the flowers were put. If a household could not grow enough roses for its own use in the seventeenth century then it supplemented supplies by buying bushels of roses from the market. Acres of roses were grown commercially throughout the world to satisfy the demand. By Victorian times roses were forced and cajoled into blooming practically all year round to provide flowers to decorate ball gowns or dinner tables. Grand ladies might weigh down their silk-taffeta evening dresses with bushfuls of tea-roses, picked from heated greenhouses, to last just one night.

Rose-water has been used as a lotion for sore and dry skin since it was first produced in Persia in the tenth century. Distilled rose-water is still an important flavouring ingredient in many middle-eastern dishes. Roses have long been considered to have healing properties. As they were also very pleasurable they have remained in use while many less agreeable herbal concoctions have vanished without trace. It is easy to make a lotion from an infusion of garden rose petals but impossible to make at home something that equates with the triple-distilled rose-water available from a pharmacist. Rose essential oil cannot be made at home either. It is one of the most costly fragrance oils to produce commercially. Tons of rose petals are needed to make quite small quantities of the pure essence. Although rose essential oil is still used in some very high quality perfumes, many perfumiers now choose to use synthetic flower fragrances to keep their costs down.

Deep-red roses are generally the best colour choice if they are to be used for pot-pourris and rose-based recipes. Not all dark-red, modern varieties have a strong scent, however, though many of the old-fashioned red roses do. If you are ordering from a catalogue, check whether a rose is well-scented first.

SIMPLE ROSE-WATER

For this traditional skin-freshener use red petals if possible, which will slightly colour the water. Yellow or pink roses turn it an unappealing brown.

METHOD

Take 450 grams (1 pound) fresh, red, scented rose petals and put in an ovenproof casserole. Pour over enough still mineral water to cover them. Put a lid on the casserole and place it in a hot oven at 230°C (450°F). Leave to come to the boil then simmer for about 15 minutes. Take out of the oven and leave to cool. Strain the liquid through muslin and pour into small bottles. Keep refrigerated and use quite quickly as a skin-freshener or to treat sore or sunburnt skin. Combine it half and half with witch hazel to make a more astringent skin tonic.

MELROSETTE

A deliciously scented honey to spread on scones or to make tiny sandwiches to eat with summer fruit compotes. Quite easy but incredibly sticky to make.

METHOD

In a food processor put three cupfuls of clean, dry, red or pink scented rose petals. Process until shredded. Meanwhile stand a 450-gram (1-pound) jar of mild-tasting, clear honey in a pan of very hot water and leave to warm up and flow freely. Put spoonfuls of honey one at a time into the processor and whizz until blended. Add more honey until you have a thickish paste. Add a few drops of lemon juice, mix well then scrape everything out into small jars. Seal and keep in a cool place.

ROSE-SCENTED BEADS

The old idea of making beads impregnated with a scent to be worn next to the skin can be copied in several ways. The early versions were made from waxes and resins. An eighteenth-century recipe used gum benzoin, storax and labdanum – a sticky resin from the plant *Cistus ladaniferus*, collected originally from the coats of wild goats that had brushed against the sticky leaves – all heated together then pounded to a paste with civet and musk added. The resulting paste was rolled between hands wetted with rose-water into little beads, which were strung onto fine cord. It is possible to make beads from rose petals alone as long as they are very scented and deep red or deep pink. This idea can really only be tried during the summer when scented garden roses are in full bloom and available in large quantities.

METHOD

You will need enough red rose petals to fill a medium-sized, lidded, ovenproof casserole. Snip off each little white crescent on the petals. Pack the petals in quite tightly and pour over enough water just to cover them. Bring the pan to the boil then remove from the heat immediately. Put the lid on and place in a cool oven so that the petals are cooked gently but never boiled. Leave them for about an hour and a half. Take out of the oven, stir well then leave to cool overnight. The next day do the same again and continue for two more days after this. You will then have a dark, murky mixture, which can be chopped and mashed to a kind of paste. Take small pieces of the paste and squeeze and roll them into balls. They will shrink quite a lot on drying. Leave them to dry and, before they are hard, push a needle though them to make a hole and thread them onto a piece of string or thread. Hang this necklace in a warm place to dry completely, occasionally twisting the beads to keep them free of the thread and each other. They will dry to a dark maroon colour, almost black, and keep their faint rose aroma. Try threading them alternately with ordinary beads or bright twists of thread.

Roses indoors

Roses make good cut flowers and are one of the mainstays of the florist shop. They need a little preparation, though, if they are to do their best and not suddenly wilt or drop their petals. Most roses have tough, woody stems, which should be split a little way up from the bottom to allow them to drink water more freely. Always cut the stem at a long slant to expose the maximum surface area to the water and peel back a little of the outer bark. Remove any thorns that will get entangled with other stems or spear the flower-arranger. If there is time before arranging or using the roses, try to stand them in

Most roses, apart from some of the single and wild varieties, last well as cut flowers in arrangements. With careful treatment they should last for several days. Here a mixture of garden roses, old and new, have been cut to make a tiered basketful.

warm water for as long as possible, even overnight. Always pick roses from the garden during the evening or early morning before the sun is high. At these times the plant is less likely to wilt as it is not transpiring and losing moisture into the air and the plant cells are turgid with water. When you finally arrange the roses into their container, give them lukewarm, not icy cold, water to drink.

PINKS AND CARNATIONS

Pinks and carnations belong to the plant genus *Dianthus*, which comprises about 80 species of perennial, biennial and annual flowers. They are hardy plants of the northern temperate zone and among them are found some of the most scented and pretty garden flowers. The ancient Greeks named the plant dianthos or flower of Jove and it was used to make garlands and coronets. This is probably where the name carnation came from.

The colour range is confined to white, cream, pink and red but within this there is a fantastic variety and subtlety of shades. Knowing which plant fits into which category is quite difficult. Dianthus or pinks are basically the perennial, hardy, low-growing plants with mats of blue-grey spiky foliage that generally flower in mid-

A small-flowered, old-fashioned dianthus growing in a cottage garden through a pink erodium. The dianthus is probably 'Waithman Beauty' with its distinctive small, clock-face markings.

summer. Sweet William is the common name for a type of dianthus grown as a biennial in borders and for picking as a cut flower. Carnations have longer flower stems and larger flower-heads and some types are less hardy than pinks.

Through the centuries, the many wild species in the family have been crossed and improved to offer numerous good garden plants. *Dianthus caryophyllus* probably reached England from France around the time of the Norman Conquest and was the plant from which hardy border carnations were derived. The French called the flower 'giroflier' because it had a clove-like perfume. This term came to be used later for many other flowers with a clove scent so that the name gillyflower was widely used for differing flowers, but it usually meant carnation or pink to most people. In Tudor times, some types were used to flavour wine. The name 'sops-in-wine' was invented for a particularly strong-smelling, dark-red clove pink. The spicy scent of pinks and carnations is a delight in the garden, especially on warm, still days. Paths and borders were traditionally edged in the neat little cushions of foliage over which danced the wiry-stemmed flowers. They are still very evocative and old-fashioned and a lovely link with the gardening past.

Dianthus in general love well-drained limestone soils and thrive in sun, though a few types prefer shade. The perennial kinds are quite easy to propagate from cuttings to ensure a good supply of fresh, young plants, though old plants will last for years if kept neat and the dead flowers are removed. Sweet Williams should be planted out in autumn from bought plants or from your own plants grown from seed sown in early summer. They overwinter as small plants then bloom early the following summer. There are double kinds and single kinds and they are generally sold in mixed colours though most are within a range of scarlet, crimson, maroon, pinks and whites. Although they are cottagey and unsophisticated, they add colour and scent to the garden for weeks and need little staking or special care. They make good cut flowers with their strong, stiff stems, velvety flowers and sweet perfume and are very useful to fill in empty spaces among mixed flower borders and beds.

Tudor pots of pinks

In Tudor times, and probably well before, pinks and carnations were grown in pots and stood in gardens as a pretty focal point. It is an excellent way of growing many of these plants which, with their neat, hummocky growth, seem to suit life in a pot very well. Terracotta as a pot material looks good with the steely blue-green of the pinks' foliage.

A little structure of twigs in the Tudor fashion keeps the long, bendy stems under control. This treatment could be used on all kinds of other plants but it is particularly suitable for those with low-growing leaves and tall flower stems that need support.

To do this successfully, put young plants into the pots before the

Left. *The finished twig structure working as a support for a full-grown plant. The tall and rather weak flower stems are kept under some control using this device.*

Above. *A simpler version of the same twig structure using decorative red-barked dogwood (Cornus).*

flower stems are too tall so that they can be encouraged and threaded through the lattice work as they grow. Use young, bendy twigs of growing hazel or willow without side branches or leaves if possible. Start with the tallest middle twigs in a cross pushing the stems down deep into the soil at the sides of the pot then continue adding the rest of the twigs progressively shorter and as evenly spaced as possible. The twigs should be clear of the plant's roots. You can tie the twigs with raffia or plant twine at strategic points to keep everything firm if you wish. Do not worry if your first attempt is a little wobbly as it is the kind of thing that takes practice to do really well. It also requires a good choice of twigs of equal thickness and straightness, which are not always easy to find.

A pot of pinks in this style would look lovely in the centre of a formal herb garden, on a terrace, standing either side of a gateway or a door, or at the beginning or end of a neat brick path. Every fortnight or so feed the pots with a weak solution of a liquid fertilizer to keep the plants growing and healthy. Trim away any straggly stems and foliage to retain a neat appearance and outline.

MORE POTS OF SCENTS

Growing scented plants in pots and containers is a useful way of putting scent exactly where you want it in the garden and gives you the opportunity to bring it indoors even if it is just for a short stay.

In early summer, plant a few seeds of the highly scented white morning glory *Ipomoea alba* or Moon flower. When the plants are beginning to climb, plant them into pots of three or more and make a structure for them to scramble and twine up. This can be made from canes or twigs (see page 26) or a ready-made metal framework. In a cold summer they can be slow to get going and, in any case, will not flower until quite late in the season. The enormous, white, trumpet blooms open in the evening and close before midday. They are excellent in a conservatory or greenhouse too.

Small pots of the insignificant little plant mignonette *Reseda lutea* were traditionally grown for the purpose of scenting rooms. They were stood on a windowsill and the current of air from the open window wafted the sweet scent inside. Few people grow this plant these days as it is in no way showy or very attractive with its little spires of rusty-green flowers and small, dull-green leaves. It is an easy annual, however, and seems happy grown in a container so it is worth sowing seed early in the year for late-spring flowering or at any time thereafter for correspondingly later blossoming. A succession of plants would not be too difficult to organize.

Now is the time to plant out nicotiana plants near windows and into moveable pots for flowering in a few weeks' time. Slugs and snails find the young plants irresistible, particularly when they are confined in pots, so be warned and arm yourself with whatever you use to deter them. White *Nicotiana officinalis* probably looks best

The elegantly shaped flowers of white nicotiana compensate for the plant's tendency to become quite tall and ungainly. Dwarf versions are bred to overcome this problem but they lose out on fragrance. Here Nicotiana affinis *combines well with other summer bedding plants.*

massed on its own as it can grow quite tall but if you want to combine it with other plants for a more interesting effect, think about using it alongside white cosmos or with the white candytuft *Iberis amara* 'Giant Hyacinth – Flowered White' or antirrhinums in any single colour. Some foliage plants added to the nicotiana, such as grey felted helichrysum or one of the senecios, make a good combination and foil.

SUMMER-SCENTED BORDERS

Although fragrance is unlikely to be the main criterion when choosing plants for a border or area of garden it should always be an important consideration, particularly when you are planning to plant near the house or around a seating area. It is equally important to avoid plants that smell unpleasant or attract unwelcome insects.

Summer scents can be roughly divided into day-time and night-time scents and there are some that are most obvious after rain or when the air is humid. Not many flowers emit fragrance that carries a long way on the air as most scents are held within the flower or leaves, though some just need to be brushed against or moved to release scent. Warm, still days are most conducive to the enjoyment of plant fragrances, and areas of garden contained by walls, tall hedges or other barriers provide the best conditions of all. If you do not have these kinds of boundaries, it is easy enough to construct something that can do the job, such as a trellis or a fence. Using scented climbers can add to the fragrant effect.

Honeysuckles

Many of the climbing honeysuckles *Lonicera* are scented, though some of the more exotic-flowered ones have no scent at all. The fragrance of some honeysuckles carries on the air during the daytime and is even stronger at night. A few kinds of honeysuckle are an absolute must in the scented garden. An early variety, which is the first to kick off the season, is Early Cream. It will sprawl up a fence or tree or can be grown on a stake to create a cascading umbrella of flowers. The trumpet flowers are cream-coloured and strongly scented, particularly at night, which is when they are visited by moths for pollination. The wild hedgerow honeysuckle *L. periclymenum* has one of the finest scents and it flowers a little later along with *L. × americana*, a North American semi-evergreen hybrid with a spicy perfume that can reach 10 metres (30 feet) in height. A honeysuckle with a less-showy flower is *L. japonica*, the Japanese honeysuckle, which is evergreen and has tiny, tubular flowers set in among the foliage. The white flowers, which yellow with age, have a penetrating and delicious lemony fragrance. It is an excellent climber to smother an ugly fence or building. *L. etrusca* is a little more difficult to grow, needing several years to settle down

Several different honeysuckle varieties flowering during the early summer. Wild honeysuckles are woodland and hedgerows plants so bear this in mind when planting them in a garden. They all thrive with their roots growing in deep, moist soil. The flowering shoots clamber up through a host plant or support to bloom with their heads in the dappled sun.

75

before flowering and sometimes succumbing to cold weather. A semi-evergreen from the Mediterranean, it has gloriously scented creamy-yellow flowers. All these scented climbing honeysuckles love to grow with their feet in the shade in good, rich soil and to let their heads flower up in the sun.

Herbaceous Perennials

There are many summer herbaceous plants with scents that just have to be included in a scented garden. Sweet rocket or dame's violet *Hesperis matronalis* is one of those old-fashioned, cottagey, perennial garden plants that have recently come back into favour. Still seen growing wild along river banks and damp hedgerows, it is a member of the wallflower family and has the same simple, cruciform flowers in clusters along a tall stem. The flowers are either pure white or soft mauve and have a violet perfume that intensifies at night with clove-like undertones. Gerard described the dame's violet as having 'great large leaves of a dark green colour, snipt about the edges . . . the flowers come forth at the top of the branches, like those of the stock gillyflower, of a very sweete smell'. They were considered the best of all the clove-scented flowers.

There is a rarer double form of dame's violet called 'Double White Rocket', which is simply a must in any all-white scented border. It is propagated by cuttings and has a scent even more powerful than that of other forms of dame's violet. Happily it is available once again after many years of horticultural neglect. Sow seed of the single version in spring and the next year the plants will flower. Patches or drifts of several plants together look lovely as a pale contrast to other, more colourful border plants.

Phlox are good-natured, easy-to-grow herbaceous perennials. They demand moist soil and the whole plant needs to be split every few years. They have a subtle and spicy scent, most noticeable when the flowers are picked and brought indoors. Certain colours have better scents than others and they can all develop an unpleasant smell as the flowers fade. Stocks have the same problem. In their case it is generally caused by the stems rotting under water and adding a nasty cabbage smell to their sweet, clove perfume.

Stocks come from a complicated genus of plants (*Matthiola*) which, like dame's violet, is related to wallflowers. There are species and varieties that flower all year round as well as smaller annual kinds and some perennial ones. The type known as ten-week stock can be flowering just ten weeks after the seed has been sown. The diminutive annual *Matthiola bicornis*, or night-scented stock, is the kind of seed-packet flower included in childrens' flower-garden mixtures. Easy and quick to grow, it makes a patch of mauve and off-white flowers that emit a heavy and exotic night-time scent, coming and going in elusive waves. *Matthiola elliptica* is a perennial, low, shrubby bush with pure-white, highly scented flowers. It is a neat little shrub for a mixed, scented border.

The clean, white flowers of dame's violet, or sweet rocket. Grown together with the mauve version they look good in large clumps at the back of a border or in an informal part of the garden. Dusk on a still day is the best time to appreciate their wonderful fragrance.

Edgers and fillers

The front of any garden border always needs special planning and attention. Choose low-growing or even creeping and sprawling plants for this site. Lavenders grown on the edges and ends of borders fit in well with other plants. Right at the front of beds, low-growing, bushy thymes and other herbs, such as hyssop and marjoram, make good, scented edgers. Keep the creeping thymes, mints and chamomiles to plant among paving or paths where they will be walked upon and then release their lovely, warm, herby scents. In medieval times, little raised seats were made from turf or herbs such

Above. *Long-stemmed stocks are well-loved cut flowers. They come in a really good range of colours, from deep burgundy, mauve, pink and white to a warm, creamy yellow. Here they are a brilliant cerise pink.*

Right. *A bunch of summer flowers drink water from a bucket before being taken indoors to fill bases and bowls. The palest, softest colours combine with pink-edged sweet peas, 'Doris' pinks and mauve scabious.*

as thyme to provide soft and fragrant places to rest awhile. It is an idea that could be copied today.

Town gardens with no beds or borders and everything planted into containers can still get the scented treatment. Many herbs, scented foliage plants and even larger shrubs, such as rosemary, lemon verbena and lavender, are perfectly happy growing in a limited space. Their proximity to garden seats and tables means that you can enjoy touching them easily and releasing all the different scents around you. Even in small town gardens it is possible to grow tubs containing sweet peas, night-scented stocks and all the other good things. It means, however, that you will need to plan carefully, including dramatic, decorative plants to make up for any less-visually interesting plants, such as the *Matthiola bicornis*.

NIGHT-SCENTED FLOWERS

Soft, warm summer evenings are a special occasion. The light is just fading but it is still pleasant enough to remain outside, light lamps or candles and perhaps slowly finish a meal surrounded by scents and pale flowers. Even though there may be few perfect nights like this in any one summer, it is good to plan for the possibility and be sure that the surroundings come up to scratch to meet the mood of the evening. Nicotiana is a must, either in pots or in flower borders, as is night-scented stock (see pages 76 and 78).

Heliotrope is a particularly lovely plant to grow in summer containers, either alone or mixed with other plants. Its common name is cherry pie, which describes the warm almond and fruit fragrance of the mauve, purple or white flowers. The rough leaves are dark-green with a silvery sheen and the flowers are formed in tight clusters, a little like those of a purple buddleia. *Heliotropium peruvianum* is quite a popular type. It is sold as a small plant early in the summer for bedding out, and sometimes as a larger standard or shrub-sized plant. There are numerous different named varieties and the paler-mauve-flowered varieties seem to have the strongest scent. The rich, deep purples are the most attractively coloured flowers but are not quite as scented. *H. peruvianum* was very popular in Victorian times, used as a bedding plant in large quantities and as a conservatory plant throughout the year. It can be grown from seed so plant it straight into a bed outdoors or keep it in a pot or container. Bear in mind, though, that it is not hardy, so overwinter stock plants in a frost-free place or take cuttings to keep for the following year.

The white Californian tree poppy *Romneya coulteri* is a good terrace plant happy growing in the small spaces between paving stones, though the stems can grow up to 1.5 metres (5 feet) high. It has huge, papery, white petals, surrounding a golden boss of stamens and is only fragrant at night. Many night-scented flowers are white, which means there is a double benefit of being able to smell their fragrance and see their pale, ghostly shapes in the garden at dusk.

A small enclosed space, such as a paved courtyard, is the best possible location for night-scented flowers. A standard hibiscus fills the air with its cherry fragrance, which combines with scent from daturas, nicotiana and citrus blossom.

Summer jasmine has to be included for its incomparable scent and tiny, delicate, starry, white flowers. Another climber, but this time less hardy than the jasmine, is the evergreen *Trachelospermum*. The leaves are small, neat and glossy and it is a good, though not commonly grown, wall plant. There are two highly scented types: *T. jasminoides* and *T. asiaticum*. While they are generally hardy, they ideally need the protection of a wall. They flower quite late in the summer with a very similar scent to jasmine.

All scented lilies release their perfume even more generously at night. When the air is still the scents of roses, honeysuckles and many other climbing plants are more obvious than during the day. The strangely exotic and wonderful daturas have magnificent night-time scents. From the nightshade family, they are sub-tropical and therefore tender and at one time were seen only in conservatories and greenhouses. They seem to be enjoying a new role as container plants for the summer garden. The white-flowered kinds are the most scented, though there are also scented varieties with mauve and yellow flowers. *Datura suaveolens*, a Mexican species that can be raised from seed and is suitable for growing in a container, is probably the most popular species. All parts of datura plants are poisonous but the wonderful scent from the enormous trumpet flowers is reminiscent of narcissi and Madonna lilies.

By the middle of summer onwards the huge flowers of *Magnolia grandiflora* begin to bloom in succession among the large, glossy leaves. A big-shrub or tree most often seen planted against a high wall or building, this is not a plant for small gardens. The vast, exotic flowers unfurl their thick, creamy petals and their scent carries on the air in a remarkable way. It has been claimed that it can be detected up to a mile away. The scent was once described as being 'the most agreeable odour which at one moment reminds us of the jasmine or lily of the valley, the next of the violet mixed with the apricot'. It is certainly stunning – rich but lemony – and it is a great treat to pick one perfect bloom and float it in a dish of water as a lovely flower arrangement. Do not touch the petals, however, as, like gardenias, they rapidly turn brown once handled or bruised.

Summer Perfumes

On hot, dusty summer days a cooling splash of flower-scented water or perfume quickly refreshes and revives. Somehow the perfume of flowers is what we crave, not the richer and more exotic scents of animal or resin origin.

A magnificent display of lavender flowers from L. stoechas pedunculata. *The flower tips have long bracts like tiny pennants, quite unlike the normal lavender varieties. This plant is particularly suited to the front or corner of a border. Here it edges some steps.*

Flower scents suit the daytime and are never heavy or overpowering. Many herb fragrances are also delicious used in lotions and toilet waters. Some have a healing or soothing property for the skin as well as a pleasant effect on the senses. An infusion of sage leaves is believed to calm sunburnt skin while rosemary is cleansing and antiseptic. Lavender water, a classic cooling lotion, was used at one time to dab on the wrists and temples. Eau-de-Cologne was considered a perfectly respectable, discreet toilet water in the days when most perfumes were thought to be a little doubtful used too lavishly.

SUMMER SPLASH-ON WATER

These days it is not possible to buy medicinal alcohol so vodka has to do as the medium in which to carry the scents.

INGREDIENTS

1 cup fresh rose petals
½ cup fresh lavender heads
4 whole cardamom pods, crushed
150 millilitres (⅓ pint) vodka (highest proof possible)
70 millilitres (⅛ pint) spring water
20 drops bergamot essential oil
20 drops orange essential oil
15 drops lemon essential oil
10 drops rose geranium essential oil

METHOD

Put the essential oils into the vodka and stir thoroughly. Cover and leave to stand for two days. Heat the spring water to boiling and pour it over the rose petals and lavender. Leave to cool. Strain the water then mix in the vodka and put in the crushed cardamom pods with seeds. Pour the mixture into a jar or bottle and cork tightly. Leave for up to four weeks, shaking occasionally. Finally, strain through a coffee filter-paper and rebottle. You can dilute it with more spring water if you would prefer the scent to be weaker. Use it to splash over the body after bathing or showering.

INSECT DETERRENTS

Summer days mean that there are lots of biting and stinging insects around. Fortunately, there are all kinds of natural ways in which scent can be used to deal with the problem. The first line of attack is to try to dissuade them from getting too near you in the first place. The blends of essential oils described here act as an effective deterrent when dabbed on to wrists, ankles and other vulnerable areas of exposed skin. Use either the water-based or oil-based lotion, according to your preference.

Insect oil

Add 10 drops of lavender essential oil and 10 drops of peppermint essential oil to 20 millilitres (¾ fluid ounce) of almond oil.

Insect lotion

Add 5 drops of lemongrass essential oil, 5 drops of lavender essential oil and 5 drops of peppermint essential oil to 3 tablespoons of witch-hazel. Mix well then add up to 12 tablespoons of water.

If you are stung or bitten by midges or mosquitoes, dab neat lavender essential oil or a mixture of chamomile and lavender oils on to the bite. For wasp stings, treat the wound first with wine vinegar to neutralize the alkalinity then proceed with the oil treatment.

LAVENDER CELEBRATION

While the scent of summer roses is romantic, soft and even exotic, the fragrance of lavender in contrast is brisk, clean and astringent. Powerfully evocative, it brings back memories of linen-cupboards, old-fashioned soaps and cottage gardens filled with the big, billowy plants sprawling over brick paths. Lavender attracts bees and butterflies to its swaying stems and, though a plant from southern Europe enjoying heat and tolerant of poor soils, varieties of it are happy in less sunny climates.

It has always been the wash-day herb, adding its fresh scent to white linen since the time when clothes and sheets were pounded and scrubbed at streamsides. Washing was draped across the growing lavender bushes, which provided a perfect scented support to the rough, homespun sheets and shirts while they aired. Dried and crumbled into little bags, lavender has always been slipped among stored fabrics to keep them fresh and insect-free. Loose lavender-heads were also used for the same purpose, either alone or mixed with other ingredients, such as spices and fixatives, and ground into sweet powders. Lavender is still grown as a commercial crop today to provide the raw material for the perfume industry and dried flower-heads for pot-pourris and sachets.

However small your garden is, and unless it is in deepest shade, try to grow at least one lavender bush. There are many types to choose from, including dwarf varieties suitable for a small garden. The most highly scented tend to come from the larger types of the old English lavenders *Lavandula spica* such as 'Grappenhall' or 'Seal' varieties. If you are searching for the deepest purple flowers, try 'Hidcote' variety or 'Twickle Purple'. The most dwarf kind is *L. nana compacta* in a mauve version called 'Munstead', and there is a tiny, neat, white-flowered version of *nana* called *alba*. The dwarf types make a lovely little scented edging or hedge if kept clipped.

Lavenders should always be trimmed back a little after flowering to remove any dead flower spikes and a little of the year's growth of foliage. Never cut back into old wood, though, as the plant will probably not reshoot from it. Lavenders are not the longest living of plants and will need to be replaced after several years, but keeping them under control gives them a longer life. Harvesting lavender for use indoors should be done when the tiny flowers are just reaching maturity. The little petals will shrivel as the flower dries, leaving the tiny, seed-like base of the flower, which we tend to think of as the flower itself. Pick stems on a fine, dry day in mid-morning when the perfume is most pronounced. Hang them in small bunches to dry out of direct sun and then strip the 'seeds' off the stems. Keep the stems to burn on an open fire in winter and scent the room.

Lavender can be used to make subtle-tasting cakes and puddings. Ice-creams and sorbets are particularly good as the scent and flavour of the flower still comes through the icy sweetness. One way of using the flavour of lavender is to grind up the dried flowers with

A bunch of very fresh lavender with each tiny flower at its best. These wither and leave the small seeds, which are used as dried lavender. Always pick lavender on a dry day and when the flowers are most open.

A powerfully fragrant mixture of different foliage to use in the kitchen. It is sensible to have a fresh jugful ready to be used at any time. Included are stems of ginger mint, apple mint, lemon verbena and eau-de-Cologne mint.

INGREDIENTS FOR
TISANES
Pot-marigold flowers
Chamomile flowers
Lemon verbena leaves
Mint leaves
Bergamot flowers and
leaves
Borage flowers and leaves
Rose flowers
Violet flowers
Angelica leaves and stems
Sweet cicely flowers

sugar and to store this mixture to use for sweetening anything that would be enhanced by it. Or you can simply bury a few whole stems in a jar of sugar in the way that you might with vanilla pods.

LAVENDER SORBET

This is simply a recipe for lemon sorbet using an infusion of fresh lavender flowers as flavouring. It makes enough for four. Serve in small glasses decorated with a sprig of flowering lavender.

INGREDIENTS

450 millilitres (¾ pint) water
125 grams (4½ ounces) castor
  sugar
Pared rind and juice of 2
  lemons
6 stems fresh lavender flowers

METHOD

Dissolve the castor sugar in water in a saucepan. Bring to the boil and simmer for five minutes. Throw in the lavender flowers and lemon rind then remove from the heat and leave to infuse until completely cold. Strain the lemon juice into the syrup then remove the lavender and lemon peel. Pour into a container, cover and freeze for two to three hours until half frozen. Beat the mixture then return it to the freezer until firm. Soften for ten minutes in the fridge before serving. Alternatively, freeze the sorbet in an ice-cream maker for quicker and smoother results. Follow the manufacturer's instructions, which will vary from machine to machine.

COOKING WITH FLOWERS

Flowers used in recipes are usually there to add to the visual excitement of the food or to provide subtle flavours. Rose, orange-flower and elderflower perfumes are not considered strange in foods. Scent is not usually the important element though it is difficult to define where the senses of taste and smell overlap. Scent and taste combine and make a single harmonious experience in cool drinks and tisanes based around flower or herb ingredients. The American mint julep is a perfect example of scent in a glass; it packs a punch into the bargain.

Delicate flower teas or tisanes begin to work even before the first taste as you inhale the warm, soothing scent from the cup. The effect is generally relaxing, especially when made from herbs such as chamomile or flowers such as violets. It can be invigorating too if made from sharp-scented mints or spicy pot-marigold petals.

The method for making tisanes is generally the same no matter what flower or leaf you use. The water should be boiling when poured over the ingredient and the mixture left for a few minutes to infuse. Amounts are difficult to calculate but dried petals and leaves are more concentrated than fresh ones. For a tea such as melissa tea made from lemon balm, *Melissa officinalis*, use a tablespoon of torn, fresh leaves to make two cups. One tablespoon of mint would be enough, though, as it is much stronger tasting. You will have to experiment a little to find what suits you.

Make flavoured and scented syrups during the summer, based on fruits and flowers, or flowers alone, to dilute with still or sparkling water or wine for long, cooling drinks. Lemon and elderflower combine well, as do red currant and rose. A syrup scented with the leaves of black currants is delicious made into a sorbet or a refreshing drink. A dash of orange-flower water is good in any kind of orange drink, and blackcurrant syrup with an apple-mint flavouring is an unexpected but delicious combination.

SCENTED GERANIUMS

Scented geraniums belong to the fascinating *Pelargonium* genus. It is unusual because there are dozens of different plant scents within it. The fragrance is contained in the leaves, which are generally quite small and prettily shaped, some variegated, some ferny, others sticky to the touch. They make neat plants ideally suited to pot-

The leaves of scented geraniums vary enormously in their shapes and textures. Some have deeply cut or filled edges; a few are soft and downy and others sticky to the touch. It is tempting to build up a collection of all the different geranium fragrances.

85

*THE RANGE OF
PELARGONIUM SCENTS*

P. abrotanifolium. An incense perfume like southernwood.

P. 'Attar of Roses'. A strong scent of rose.

P. canescens. Grey leaves that smell like incense.

P. citriodorum. Strong lemon perfume.

P. denticulatum. Slender cut leaves with balsam scent.

P. filicifolium. Fern-shaped leaves smelling of resin.

P. 'Joy Lucille'. Peppermint scent.

P. 'Moore's Victory'. Large flowers for a scented variety. Leaves have a cayenne pepper smell.

P. nervosum. Has lime-scented foliage.

P. odoratissimum. Soft, velvety leaves smelling of green apples.

P. 'Prince of Orange'. Smells of oranges.

P. tomentosum. Has large, soft, hairy leaves and a peppermint scent.

culture and they thrive on windowsills where other plants would not. Almost all the varieties are native to South Africa and not fully hardy. They can be propagated simply from cuttings taken in late summer to provide fresh, young plants for the following year. Once the collecting bug has bitten you, you may want to make a complete collection of all the different fragrances.

The Victorians were very fond of these little plants and used their leaves to flavour cakes and puddings, to float in finger-bowls and to make scented bookmarks. A geranium leaf often partnered flowers for a buttonhole or posy, and cottage windows were usually crammed with several pots of these cheerful plants, all fighting for light in the overcrowded, dark rooms.

The leaves dry well and keep their special scents so are ideal for making pot-pourri. Pot-grown plants can be moved outdoors on to terraces and steps for the summer months or bedded out among other summer plantings until the chance of the first autumn frosts means that they should be brought back under cover. The scented-leaved pelargoniums generally have small and delicate pink, white or red flowers. There are other similar types, such as the Uniques and Regals, that often have more showy and colourful flowers, but usually slightly less interesting scents to their leaves. There are many different types of scented pelargoniums from which to choose, but the panel (*left*) lists most of the various fragrances.

SUMMER POTS FOR INDOORS

With a little planning and effort, the fragrant pleasures of summer can also be enjoyed indoors. Summer indoor gardening is the ideal solution for people without a garden and those who have to be inside for long periods. Flowering pot plants can really brighten the home during the summer months and some kinds, such as the geranium, thrive indoors all year round, given plenty of light and a fairly dry atmosphere. Any flowering plants growing in pots outdoors can be brought inside for a short time while the blooms are at their best. Most plants will not mind the change of atmosphere for a few days or even a week, but might begin to deteriorate after that.

Pots of scented lilies

Lilies are excellent for this in-and-out treatment. They start their life outdoors, where they need no special cosseting or demanding routine. Then, at the point of flowering, the whole pot can come inside and give a magnificent show. It should be placed outside again afterwards for the rest of the summer so that the bulb rebuilds its strength for the next year.

Lilies used to be thought of as either a cut flower or a garden bloom, but now you can buy them ready-potted and in flower. Although these pots are certainly convenient, they often contain

unscented varieties, which is a pity. It generally pays to plant your own bulbs in spring so that you can choose the best scented types (see pages 20-25). Plant several different varieties to stagger the flowering season through the whole summer so that something is always blooming at its best. Particularly welcome in late summer and early autumn are the highly scented lilies, such as 'Casablanca', which look sumptuous with their enormous blooms and fill the whole home with scent.

When you plant up the bulbs with a view to displaying them indoors bear in mind where they are likely to go, then plant them into suitable pots. If you intend to stand the pots in cache pots or baskets then any basic plastic version will do, otherwise use good, heavy terracotta, which looks smart enough to be left uncovered. Saucers to match are a bit of a luxury but necessary if the lilies are standing on carpets or polished floors. If you do not have glazed terracotta saucers then redundant dinner plates will stop the water or soil leaking out. Some types of lily, such as *Lilium regale*, get very tall and require staking. This means that, unless you have a very big house, they are only really suitable to stand on the floor or in a fireplace.

For several magical days the scent of Lilium regale *in full bloom will fill a house with fragrance. Grown in pots like this they are almost spectacularly showy so look best in simple surroundings.*

While the pots are indoors and the lilies are flowering you can cover the soil at the base of the stems with a little moss if you like, as you might do for hyacinths growing in bowls (see page 22). This looks prettier than bare earth and stops the earth losing moisture as quickly as it would if uncovered. When the lily flowers have faded, cut off the dead heads and put the plants back outdoors. Stand the pots out of view and in a sheltered place, allowing them to get plenty of sun but not to be scorched. Check that the leaves still look healthy. If there are aphids feeding on them, use a safe insecticide to get rid of them quickly as aphids can carry harmful lily viruses and diseases, which will rapidly attack the bulbs. Do not neglect the plants just because they have stopped looking good. Keep them watered and fed with a weekly dose of liquid fertilizer until the stems die right back after turning brown. The aim is to nurture the spent bulb and to build it up for another season.

Lilies have large and prominent stamens loaded with gingery-brown pollen when they are in full flower. If you bring lilies indoors, be careful not to brush the stamens against clothes, carpets or furnishings as the pollen has a powerful stain. If you do get pollen on something, act quickly and try to brush it off. If you wet the mark, the bright-orange stain seems to set and then nothing will remove it. Sometimes a small piece of sticky tape dabbed on to the pollen will lift it off completely. Florists usually snip out the stamens if they are using open lilies in arrangements and bouquets. This solves the pollen problem but does spoil the flowers somehow as they definitely look as if they are lacking something. You simply expect the stamens to be there.

Large-scale lilies have enormous impact in any kind of flower arrangement. They combine well with many different materials but are most effective used quite simply, such as here with greeny white Viburnum opulus *'snowballs'. Push the fresh-cut stems into damp, floral foam to support the heavy heads in a light container, such as a basket.*

SUMMER FLOWER ARRANGEMENTS AND DECORATIONS

The choice of flowers for summer arrangements is overwhelming. If you have a productive garden and grow plants specifically for their scents you will have plenty of material to make everything from tiny posies to lavish displays. Although it might seem unimportant to have flowers decorating the house when you can enjoy them outside, one of the pleasures of summer is the plenitude of flowers in bloom, so why not enjoy them to the full?

While the sweet peas are romping away producing fresh flowers every day, make the most of them and keep picking. As with all flowering annuals, their blooming will slow down if they are allowed to make seed so cutting stems is positively beneficial. You may be less inclined to pick ruthlessly from flowering shrubs and roses if they are designed to fill the garden with colour but taking a few blooms from here and there makes little difference to the overall scheme. Roses should always be deadheaded to encourage flowering, so picking them can be seen as an early version of this chore. Pick flowers from the garden with good, sharp scissors or secateurs so that you cut cleanly. Never leave ragged ends to the stems. Cut roses to the desired length, choosing a point immediately above an outward-facing leaf node and making a cut that slopes upwards and outwards. Any stem left above a leaf node will just wither and die back. This not only looks ugly but can also allow disease to enter the plant. Picking branches from shrubs and large plants for flower arrangements acts like pruning, so make use of it to shape up the plant, even if it is not the usual time of year to do it. If possible, gather material first thing in the morning or in the evening when the air is cool and plants are not transpiring. Put the cut stems into cool, not icy, water immediately and leave them if possible for a few hours to have a long drink before arranging them. Flowers bought from a market stall or flower shop should have been conditioned in this way, though it is sensible to cut the stems again at an angle once you get the flowers home, to make them take up water more easily.

Flower arrangements do not have to be elaborate or complicated and they do not need special equipment and skills. The best floral displays are those made from flowers you love or have grown yourself put into a favourite container and stood somewhere with pride. The pleasure they give is a thousand times greater than huge, formal and elaborate arrangements, which generally look quite out of place in modern homes. Speed and effect is what most people want. Nothing should take too long to put together and the result should have maximum impact without costing a fortune in flowers. The simplest arrangements are really just large posies or bunches made in the hand and stood straight into a suitable container. Jugs are ideal for these kinds of flowers. Plain glass cylinders or laboratory tanks, understated but classically stylish, suit every arrangement.

Larger arrangements might need what are known in the floristry trade as mechanics. These include floral foam or scrunched-up wire netting to hold tall or heavy stems. If you simply want to display some lovely, scented blooms in a straightforward way, you generally will not need any of this. The current fashion in flowers is for a relaxed and cottagey look. Alongside this is a taste for sophisticated but definitely simple arrangements, which depend on clever colour schemes, the subtle mixing of varieties of flowers and really well-designed containers and vases.

Arranging scented flowers is no different from using any other kinds of flowers. They will have the most effect the nearer they are to where people are likely to be, such as beside armchairs and sofas or on a dining table. A hall is a good place to stand perfumed flowers because people move through it frequently, disturbing the air and noticing the scent. Most flowers need warmth to reveal their fragrance fully. Although a kitchen will provide this, food scents are likely to smother flower fragrance. A warm, sunny room, such as a conservatory or garden room – a room with lots of glass designed for living in rather than for plants – is a perfect place to enjoy the scent from a cut-flower arrangement but do not expect the flowers to last as long as they would in a cooler, darker situation.

The summer is the one time when it is possible to make wonderfully elaborate and generous flower arrangements, which might be used for a wedding or other special occasion. Apart from the obvious roses, peonies and other garden flowers, try adding some unusual materials like tiny wild strawberry sprays or other fruits for an opulent mixture.

Autumn
A Rich Harvest

With the beginning of a chill in the air and dampness creeping up from the soil, autumn provides quite new and different scents. Fruit and ripeness are the key elements to a powerful mixture of plenty and decay but there are still memories of summer left in the fragrance of the last few roses and aromatic herbs.

The scent of apples is quite distinctive. Nothing else captures the feel of the autumn season as well. Wild hops add a strong, herbal note.

The intensely floral scents of summer mellow in autumn to a richer, deeper range of smells. The dampness in the air and the harvest of ripe fruits, fungi and other seasonal things lends a poignant edge to the fragrances. There are fewer fragrant border flowers in bloom and those there are rarely carry scent into the air. Instead there are scents of apples and quinces on the bough and windfalls on the ground. There are woodland scents of ferns and leaves and an unmistakeable overriding autumn scent, pleasant but always hinting at ripeness and inevitable decay.

Of the garden flowers still in bloom, a few have distinctive but not particularly pleasing fragrances. Chrysanthemums, for example, have a strange, pungent, spicy smell which, although very recognizable, is not generally considered a pleasant or interesting fragrance. There are, however, some attractive fragrances to be found. The lovely, evergreen myrtle shrub does not generally produce its little, fluffy, white flowers until late in the summer and on into the autumn. The whole plant has a warm, spicy, almost savoury smell, which is released if you squeeze a leaf or brush past the plant. Position it against a wall, beside an entrance, or somewhere where you can touch it regularly or pick a leaf as you pass.

Few of the large-flowered clematis have any scent. Their showy blooms, rather unusually, are formed from the sepals rather than the petals. Many of the species, however, especially those with tiny, bell-shaped flowers, do have delicious perfumes. In late summer and autumn *Clematis rehderiana* blossoms with small, hanging, dusty-yellow flowers smelling of cowslips. *Clematis flammula*, or fragrant Virgin's bower, another late flowerer, which looks similar to a wild clematis and has clusters of small, greenish-white flowers, is also magnificently perfumed. The scent is like meadowsweet and can be almost overpowering if you go near the plant. It is an excellent climber to let ramble up an old tree stump, over an arch or an ugly building as it is very vigorous.

A full-grown quince tree laden with golden fruits can scent a whole garden with its special perfume. The smell is sweet and lingering and a single fruit brought indoors will perfume a room as well as any kind of fruit left lying next to it for a while. As a garden tree the quince *Cydonia oblonga* is not commonly planted but it is a perfect choice for a small space, making a neat, rounded shape. It produces large, pale-pink flowers in spring, which look like huge apple-blossoms lying along the length of each branch. The leaves are a soft silvery-green and in autumn come the hard, golden-yellow, pear-shaped fruits with downy skins.

This old-fashioned fruit is quite delicious when made into preserves of all kinds, or mixed with apples or pears in puddings, where it imparts its unique scent and flavour. At one time there was a great choice of types and many named varieties; nowadays you will be lucky to find any more than two on offer. Look out for 'Portugal' and 'Meech's Prolific'. Plant a quince in good, rich soil with plenty of moisture and enjoy its pleasures for many years.

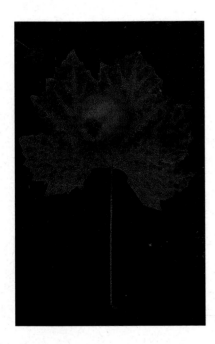

Colours in nature are as rich as scents are strong at this time of the year. A brilliantly marked vine leaf is background to a golden quince and tiny, red crab apples lying on freshly dug soil.

As the days shorten and the warmth of indoors seems more enticing than being outside, there are all kinds of tasks to be done: sorting ingredients for making pot-pourris and scented mixtures, and planning and organizing the scented garden for next year. By now few things remain to be harvested, except perhaps some decorative seed-heads and the last few summer annuals, such as cornflowers, which sometimes flower until late autumn. Old-fashioned roses often surprise by producing a marvellous crop of late flowers, so some can still be picked for their petals and for drying whole rose-heads. Most fragrant leaves will have lost their powerful scents as they begin to wither and die, but some plants such as lemon verbena can be stripped of leaves now before they turn brown and drop from the plant anyway. If the first, hard frosts come late, you may still be picking sweet peas for the house, smaller now and with short stems, but still a delight.

AUTUMN POT-POURRIS

If you have been drying and collecting materials throughout the summer, by now you should have a good choice of ingredients to finish making dry and moist pot-pourris. Now is the time when you will need to get together all the necessary extras for assembling pot-pourri mixtures such as spices, fixatives and oils.

Spices

Spices have always had a function beyond flavouring foods. Their scents have been used to freshen and cleanse the air in musty rooms, to make perfumed powders to put into cupboards and drawers and to scent perfumes. The scents of spices, like those of herbs and certain flowers, were believed to ward off disease and were used to make pomanders and wax beads carried or worn like an amulet. Spices have been used in medicine as well as the kitchen, and as preservatives and fixatives for other scents. At one time spices were as valuable as gold and even used as a kind of currency. Some of the most important trade routes of the world were developed because of the demand for spices, and in households that could afford the precious stuff, lockable spice chests were used to store them.

We are able to buy spices of all kinds these days, whole or ground. The best spices to use are as fresh as possible, ground when you need them. If you intend to use spices frequently, invest in a small, electric coffee-grinder in which you can grind whole spices to whatever degree of fineness you want. Keep the machine just for spices unless you want to risk your coffee being flavoured with cardamom or anise. A few spices, such as nutmeg, are exceptionally hard and easier to grate on a small, metal hand-grater. For crushing just a few berries or spice seeds, a heavy pestle and mortar is useful, made from traditional ceramic, wood, stone or marble.

Squash and pumpkin beneath an old medlar tree. There is almost an embarrassment of autumn riches and the rush is on to harvest, store or make use of all the garden produce.

All spices are of plant origin and come from seeds, buds, roots, bark, seed pods or stems. Many spices, such as pepper, ginger and cloves, are native to tropical climates in Asia, while others come from the West Indies and Central America. The Mediterranean area is the original homeland of many of the aromatic spice seeds such as fennel and fenugreek.

In pot-pourris and sweet powder mixtures, ground spices are often used to introduce their scent throughout the mixture. Whole spices are often included too, partly for scent and partly because so many of them are pretty and decorative. They add shapes and textures that contrast with or complement the softer ingredients, such as leaves and petals. It is perfectly possible to make a pot-pourri

Scented leaves play an important part in making pot-pourris and fragrant mixtures but are often overlooked in place of more colourful ingredients. Here there are violet leaves, lemon verbena, olive leaves and uva ursi, which are pretty enough to be used on their own or mixed with flowers and spices.

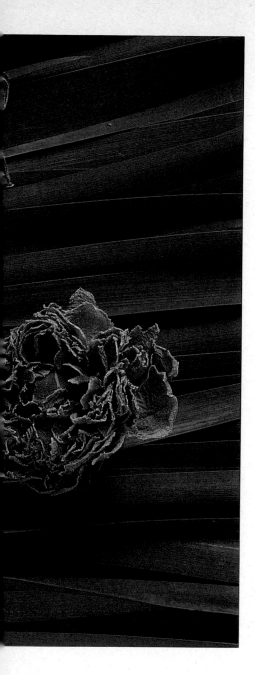

using just spices or spices and seed pods, and other materials that give the same visual feel as the spices. Small larch cones or pine cones, dried fungi, oak moss and little twigs and pieces of bark would all combine to make a woodland mixture just right for autumn. Collect odds and ends that might be suitable from all the debris of fallen leaves after autumn gales and dry everything off well before making up your mixture.

If you prefer a more exotic looking blend, combine spices – whole and ground – with decorative, dried seed pods and seeds that are widely available now and sold for this purpose. You could add colour with whole, dried chilli peppers and sweet peppers in different sizes and shapes. You can get dried baby corn, too, and strangely shaped, weird and wonderful bits of plants and stems, which all look good displayed in big, shallow bowls or baskets.

BASIC SPICE POWDER

A basic spice powder can be used for mixing with petals and leaves for making dry pot-pourris or alone in pillows, cushions and sachets. It is also the preservative and fixative used to cure citrus and clove pomanders. Look out for shops and warehouses that sell ground spices in bulk and have a quick turnover of goods. It can be very expensive to buy ground or whole spices in large quantities when you can only get them in special, fancy, little glass jars or plastic tubs. Ethnic food shops and grocers or market stalls are often the best places to buy spices at reasonable prices.

INGREDIENTS

2 cups ground cinnamon
1 cup ground cloves
½ cup ground orris root powder

¼ cup ground allspice
¼ cup ground nutmeg

METHOD

Simply combine the ingredients. This mixture can be used several times for pomanders. Store it in a tightly sealed plastic box or bag once it is mixed up.

AUTUMN SPICE POT-POURRI

This makes a coarse-textured, earthy-looking mix best displayed in an old, polished, wooden bowl or ethnic, beaten, metal dish, not fine china or glass. Vary the amount you make by adjusting the size measure that you choose. A standard teacup makes a reasonable amount. The spice powder used here is a variation on the basic spice powder on page 97.

INGREDIENTS *(continued overleaf)*

2 measures whole nutmegs
2 measures whole cloves
½ measure whole cardamom pods

½ measure mixed peppercorns: red, green, black, and white
½ measure whole star anise
½ measure ground cloves

10 large cinnamon sticks
   broken into 4 centimetre
   (1½-inch) lengths
1 measure allspice berries
1 measure mace
1 measure coriander seeds

1 measure ground cinnamon
½ measure ground orris root
¼ measure ground ginger
¼ measure crushed gum
   benzoin

METHOD

Gently mix all the main ingredients. Make up the spice powder and combine with the mixture. If you wish, you can now add other purely decorative ingredients such as seeds, seed pods and dried wood curls. You could also add an essential oil of your choice to deepen the aroma. Keep to the spice theme and choose one such as oil of cinnamon or ginger. Use only 6 to 8 drops for this amount of pot-pourri.

Oils and Essences

Before you get far into making all kinds of scented things at home, you will need to know a little about essential oils, what they are and how you use them. An essential oil or essence is an extremely concentrated form of a plant perfume taken from trees, shrubs, flowers, herbs and grasses. The perfume is extracted from the plant and held in an oil base, which can then be further diluted. Extraction is most commonly done by steam distillation but it can also be by enfleurage, maceration or expression (see page 16). Some oils are easy to extract and some plants are generous with their oils. Other oils take kilos of flowers or leaves to obtain just a few precious drops. This is why the prices of different oils vary so enormously.

There are possibly 300 or so essential oils in use today but only a small core of basic scents are used to any great degree. Essential oils are made and exported throughout the world and are used in the manufacture of many different products, from foods to medicines. Essential oils in this book are used for the scents they provide for pleasure. There is, however, a more serious side to their use. Many of these oils are very powerful. Attar of roses oil, for example, is seven times, and thyme oil twelve times, more antiseptic than old-fashioned carbolic acid. Essential oils should be handled carefully and never taken internally or put on the skin except in the case of one or two, such as lavender oil. In most cases they are used in tiny amounts, drop by drop. If oils are not sold in a dropper bottle then buy a small pipette or dropper with which to measure them out. Keep essential oils in dark-glass bottles and store them out of strong light. Always buy them from a trustworthy source.

Most oils should store for about a year without spoiling. Some oils are not pure, others do not claim to be, and there are some sold as aromatherapy oils that are already diluted with vegetable oils. These may contain pure essential oil as the fragrance or they may use chemical-based fragrances, so read the small print carefully. A good

Spices are very special ingredients to work with. They look very decorative left whole but release most scent once ground. These three bundles, from left to right, are vanilla pods, liquorice root and cinnamon. There are some nutmegs and star anise in the tin and a clove pomander beside it.

Essential oils must be stored carefully to preserve their properties. Dark-glass bottles are the traditional and best way of keeping them as fresh as possible for the greatest length of time. Buying oil in small quantities also helps.

indication of genuine oils is when their prices vary from one fragrance to another. They are much easier to find these days since the surge in popularity of aromatherapy and scented massages and all the therapeutic uses now made of essential oils.

If you are using essential oils for home-made perfumes and pot-pourris it is sensible to have a small range of different ones from which to choose. Depending on your taste, you could make a basic kit of several oils that you are likely to use most often. If you get more interested in the whole subject, you will probably want to add more later. The oils listed in the panel (*right*) are a good start.

Many other scents, such as those from herbs and spices are easily extracted from the actual plants so you may never need to use their equivalent essential oil. For massage, the oils are always diluted first in an oil carrier. One of the most popular is sweet almond oil. The proportion of a single essential oil or mixtures of more than one to the carrier oil should always be 5 to 6 drops to 10 millilitres (⅓ fluid ounce) of vegetable oil. A few people are sensitive to certain oils: cassia, thyme, cinnamon and clove, for example.

CUSHIONS AND PILLOWS

Scented cushions and pillows can be as lavish or as discreet as you like. One scented cushion among a pile of plain ones is subtle and under-stated and is what one might choose for a sitting-room sofa, conservatory basket chairs or a similar living space. A bedroom could benefit from several different scents used in pillows and cushions piled on to a bed or chair, releasing a gentle scent to freshen and perfume the room. Essential oils are useful to scent wadding or small pieces of cotton wool, which can be tucked into sachets, cushions or sleep pillows. The other, more traditional, filling is a

USEFUL ESSENTIAL OILS
Bergamot
Cedarwood
Citronella
Lemongrass
Lavender
Lime
Orange
Patchouli
Petitgrain
Rose geranium
Rosemary
Vetivert
Ylang ylang
If you can afford them:
Jasmine
Neroli
Rose

scenting powder or mixture of flowers, herbs, spices and fixatives. You can make a fine powder to fill close-weave fabric sachets or you can leave petals and leaves whole and make a coarser mixture for large pillows and cushions. The simplest version of this idea is a pillow filled with dried hops, which is believed to relax and soothe you to sleep. Sweet woodruff is another good herb for cushions. In both cases it is sensible to pull the leaves off their dried and spiky stems. Make a small inner sachet to contain the herb then slide this inside a cushion or pillow cover with the cushion padding. A good mixture for easy breathing during a cold or to help a blocked nose is made from dried eucalyptus leaves and spearmint with a little menthol essential oil added.

You could use any pleasing pot-pourri mixture to scent a cushion or pillow if you do not feel that it is a waste to hide from view all your lovingly collected ingredients. If the cushions or pillows are meant to be put among others, on a bed during the day, for example, lavender is a good choice of filling as its scent is fresh and airy.

To make a scented powder for small sachets, ideal to put into drawers and among airing linen or stored clothes, use this basic recipe. If time is short or you do not know how to sew little bags to put this in, simply put a scoop of the mixture on a small, square handkerchief, bring all the edges up together and tie a ribbon around it to make a little pouch.

Small, scented cushions can be piled up with the unscented kind. You could also make a neat pocket on a large cushion and slip a miniature scented sachet inside.

Using scraps of exotic silks to make these bags and sachets for sweet powder gives them an instantly glamorous look. You could, however, use any closely woven fabric, depending on the cushion's ultimate purpose.

SWEET POWDER FOR SACHETS

INGREDIENTS

½ cup cedar shavings
½ cup lavender
1 cup dried rose petals
½ cup dried lemon-peel
½ cup ground cinnamon
½ cup ground allspice

¼ cup ground cloves
1 cup ground orris root powder
¼ cup sugar
Few drops rose geranium or
    lemongrass essential oil

METHOD

The dry ingredients can be mixed together and used as they are or you could grind the larger ingredients in a food processor to make them finer. The cedar shavings may have to stay large unless you snip them or have managed to find them already cut up small. Add the essential oil after mixing and stir around well to disperse it.

LAVENDER MIXTURE FOR SACHETS

This makes a warm but fresh-smelling mixture ideal for putting in wardrobes, cupboards and drawers.

INGREDIENTS

2 cups dried lavender
½ cup lemon verbena leaves
½ cup dried orange-peel

¼ cup ground orris root
    powder
¼ cup ground nutmeg
Few drops orange essential oil

METHOD

Combine the dry ingredients. As with the previous recipe, the larger ingredients may be ground in a food processor if you wish to achieve a finer mixture. Add the essential oil at the end making sure it is thoroughly dispersed.

CLEAN SCENTS

Many chemically based cleaning products used in the home are given fragrances to enhance their appeal. Perfumes are added to all kinds of things that do not need them in a marketing ploy to make us feel good about what we use, to stir up memories or make connections with real ingredients that are no longer used these days. The classic pine smell, once so commonly included in disinfectants and cleaning agents, is as often as not added as a chemical, bornyl acetate. People associate the resin scent with cleanliness and the outdoors, but although the true plant extract might have antiseptic properties, the chemical version does not. Lemon has the same kind of associations with freshness and all things clean while lavender, one of the oldest household herbs, still finds its way into modern silicone wood polishes. In many cases we have lost the true reason for using a plant extract and introduce into products any fragrance that is deemed new and fashionable. Vague new scents such as 'outdoor' or 'fresh' leave us to make our own connections.

Essential oils can be used in all sorts of ways to scent the house. Real herbs and flowers still have a place too, providing a natural and often inexpensive alternative to the army of chemical household products on any supermarket shelf. Instead of unpleasant artificial scents use essential oils impregnated into wood shavings or cotton wool to freshen a room or the inside of cupboards and drawers. Try cedarwood or sandalwood for storerooms and wardrobes or rose, bergamot or ylang ylang for a bedroom. A tiny piece of cotton wool dabbed with a sharp scent, such as lemongrass or rosemary, can be

Tiny cedarwood shapes and wood shavings are impregnated with cedarwood oil and then put among clothes and linens in cupboards and drawers. As the scent fades simply replenish it with a drop or two more oil.

put into the dust-bag of a vacuum cleaner to great effect and the same oil diluted into water can be sprayed on to clothes and bed linen before ironing.

An infusion of mint or thyme leaves is an excellent wipe for kitchen surfaces, freshening everything and, in the case of thyme, cleaning with a mild disinfectant. Simply pour boiling water over fresh or dried leaves as if making a tisane, leave to cool, then strain and bottle the mixture.

SCENTED FABRIC CLEANER

Try using this mixture if you occasionally need a dry cleaner for carpets or old but precious textiles. It is suitable for anything made from fabric that is difficult to wash. Sprinkle the scented powder over the material, brush or work in well and leave overnight before vacuuming.

INGREDIENTS

4 tablespoons borax or fuller's earth or bicarbonate of soda
8 drops rosemary essential oil

8 drops lavender essential oil
4 drops bergamot essential oil

METHOD

Mix all the ingredients together well and then use.

CITRUS BATH MIX

This is for when you want a fresh and invigorating scented bath. It does not claim to do anything to your skin but smells wonderful. Run a hot bath with one sachet in it and swirl it around and squeeze it a little to release the scents. If you do not mind sharing your bath with bits then you can just throw it straight in.

INGREDIENTS

1 cup dried-milk powder
1 cup fine oatmeal
2 cups dried lemon verbena leaves, crumbled
½ cup dried lemon peel

4 dried bay leaves, crumbled
4 sprigs dried rosemary, crumbled
8 drops lemongrass essential oil

METHOD

Mix the dry ingredients together then add the oil drop by drop stirring very well. Store in an airtight jar or put into muslin sachets.

PLANNING AND PLANTING
WINTER AND SPRING BULB DISPLAYS

To have bulbs flowering for Christmas you need to plant them at precisely the right time so that they have long enough to develop. Although specially prepared and forced bulbs need this exact

You can throw a handful of this citrus bath mixture into the water as it is or, if you prefer, fill small muslin bags with it or use a herb-infuser as if you were making a tisane in a cup.

timing, other kinds of indoor bulbs can be treated a little more casually. If you just want to have something in flower for the house during the worst of the winter months then plant a mixture of different flower types during early to mid-autumn. Stagger their blooming time by holding some of them back in the cool once they are nearly ready to flower.

If you do want Christmas-flowering bulbs be sure to buy ones that claim to do this on the packet and follow any instructions that come with them. You can use more or less any suitable containers for indoor bulbs as long as they are big enough to hold the bulbs you choose. Many bulb types can be grown hydroponically on a bed of stones or other medium. If you choose to use soil there are ready-made composts designed for indoor culture or you can use any light medium such as a soil-less compost. Avoid peat-based products if possible, to help conserve stocks. If you grow bulbs in bowls and containers without built-in drainage holes, add a little ground charcoal to keep the soil sweet and prevent stagnation. Other kinds of growing media include small, round pebbles, coarse garden washed grit, marble chippings and layers of different gravel textures, both fine and coarse. You could layer up silver sand and pebbles with dark earth at the base or make stripes of dark and light pebbles. Nurseries and garden centres sell quite a few different kinds of stones and pebbles but other good sources are shops selling equipment for tropical and cold-water fish. Builders' merchants also stock this kind of thing but ensure that sand or gravel from such a source is not contaminated or mixed with things that might not suit plants.

As the growing medium can be so interesting, it seems sensible to take advantage of its visual possibilities and display everything in clear glass. Watching the roots grow down and develop from the bulbs can be as fascinating as the final flowering. Use round, glass bowls, square or rectangular laboratory tanks or old-fashioned, pressed-glass jelly moulds or dessert dishes. Any glass container can in fact be put to use except for the most precious lead crystal. Although it is rare for the glass to be spoilt during the growing process, something could react with the surface.

When planting bulbs into pebbles and stones, the bulbs can sit quite high up and do not need to be covered. They then become part of the whole effect, which is easier than trying to make them look natural as one would when planting them into soil. They need sufficient support to prevent them from falling over when they have lots of leaves and tall flower spikes. Always leave a little space between bulbs so that they are not touching each other, but they can be put closer together than you might do in the garden where they would grow bigger each year and compete for space and food.

If you are planting individual bulbs into hyacinth glasses, fill the glass with water and put the bulb on top with its base only just touching the surface of the water. This is to encourage the roots to begin growing downwards. The bulb should not be sitting too deeply in the water or it might rot before it starts to develop. A piece of charcoal in the glass will keep the water sweet.

Three of the narcissus family can be forced to flower indoors at Christmas, or later if you prefer. 'February Gold', 'Peeping Tom' and 'Tête-à-Tête' are all well-known garden types and make lovely, scented, golden bowlfuls of blooms. These varieties are probably best planted into compost and then, after flowering, can be planted out into the garden for another year. The quick-growing, bunch-flowered narcissi, such as 'Paper White', are happy to be grown in pebbles and water alone and are not suitable to be planted out as they will not survive the cold or flower again. Think of them as a one-off show only.

Take advantage of a fine autumn day and work outside preparing indoor bulbs. Small pebbles look pretty as the potting medium and are less messy than soil. Here 'Paper White' narcissi, a hyacinth and winter crocuses are being potted.

AUTUMN OUTDOOR PLANNING

Autumn is often the best time to plan ahead and make changes in the garden. The weather governs all schemes, large or small, but if the soil stays warm and is not too wet or dry, autumn is the best time to transplant growing things and to plant new ones. Plants moved in autumn will settle down well with no shocks to their system. They will be about to go into dormancy but will have enough time possibly to grow a little and be in a good state to greet the new year. Spring plantings are often caught out by sudden dry spells or wickedly cold weather, which puts them under too much extra strain. Trees and shrubs were traditionally planted during autumn. They were dug from nursery beds before the cold weather closed in and the soil became frozen or too waterlogged to work on. Nowadays many plants of all sizes are container grown and can be planted at any time of the year. Plant any important fragrant plants now, weather permitting.

The other garden jobs at this time of year are general clearing and cleaning up and protecting plants that are less than hardy. Bring indoors any tubs and pots that contain tender plants before you get caught out by a sudden, severe frost. Citrus plants and any tropical plants, such as daturas, will also need to come in. A greenhouse, glazed extension or conservatory are fine for plants that just need to be kept frost-free, but a few might need more warmth. Lilies in pots are generally happy left outdoors unless there are several days on end when the temperature is below freezing and the soil freezes through. It is best to leave them standing in a sheltered place and move them if the weather gets very cold later. Cut down dead lily stems and scrape away the top layer of soil on the pots, adding a little organic matter such as spent mushroom compost, home-made compost, or manure. Give large shrubs and trees in the garden a scattering of a slow-release, organic fertilizer, such as bone meal, and be prepared to cover scented shrubs, such as myrtle, which can suffer from cold winds that burn the foliage, turning it brown and causing it to shrivel up.

Clear away areas of annual plants in flower borders and save seeds from favourite plants. Dry seed-heads in a warm room and then shake out the seeds inside a paper bag. Store seeds in small brown envelopes. Label carefully, seal the envelopes and keep them in a dry, dark place.

If you have sown scented biennials, such as sweet Williams and wallflowers, they can be moved into their final places now ready for the spring. Plant tubs and containers with hyacinths, scented narcissi or tulips and sow fillers such as wallflowers, forget-me-nots and other spring stand-bys. You will regularly have to discard summer plants that are still flowering well to make space for the spring show. This always seems a shame. Do not leave planting bulbs too late, though tulips should not be put in until late autumn as they are the last bulbs to flower in the spring.

Some fragrant plant trimmings can be put to good use. Make bundles of lavender stems and dry them out to burn on an open winter fire. Dry and keep fennel and rosemary twigs for next season's barbecues.

Iris florentina in flower. The dried rhizome from underground is used as the fixative called orris root and it is perfectly possible to grow your own supply.

A SCENTED ARBOUR

An arbour might be rather a grand name for a place in the garden in which you sit and surround yourself in scent but it has a romantic and old-fashioned ring to it and adds inspiration to an excellent idea. No garden, of any size, can have too many seating areas. They should be in both obvious and unexpected places so that, as you turn a corner or walk behind a shed or an unlikely building, there is an inviting place to stop awhile. Arbours may be found in the place with the best view or perhaps somewhere quiet where no-one can see and disturb you. If the seat in question is wreathed about with scented climbers and shady on a hot day or protective on a wet one then so much the better.

The resting place itself can be an exquisite antique iron seat, an old-fashioned wooden park bench or a crude plank bench supported on bricks or tree stumps. It should, however, be big enough for at least two people to sit on. The structure around it for holding the plants can be as lavish or simple as your pocket can afford and your taste dictate. Whatever the supporting structure is made from, it should last as long as the plant it supports. If it does not, you will have problems, unless the plant becomes self-supporting with age. Keep in mind that as your plants grow, they will impose or ever-increasing pressure on their supports. Rustic larch-wood poles are sturdy and cheap or you could use a lattice or wattle-type woven fence or panel. You could search out some garden history books and study pictures of medieval gardens, which are full of wonderful, clever but simple structures of just this kind. Most medieval structures were made from wood such as coppiced hazel or sometimes metal. A good and imaginative local smith would be able to make a structure that could be fitted together on site, or perhaps two large metal arched rods would be enough to start some vigorous plants growing and making a curtain of scent.

Once you have the site and a basic structure, you can choose your plants. A wisteria would be lovely if you left room for the sitter among the enormous hanging panicles of flower that you would hope to get some day. Climbing honeysuckles would be perfect, especially if you mixed an early and late variety to extend the flowering season. Roses would be top of the list grown with another plant, maybe evergreen, to keep the whole thing well-clothed, which some roses might not do. A short-lived summer arbour could make use of sweet peas grown with another annual summer climber such as *Cobaea scandens*. The eglantine of Shakespeare is the deliciously scented rose species *Rosa eglanteria* or sweetbriar. It has tiny, single, pink flowers, like a wild dog rose, but the ferny foliage is scented like fresh, green apples. It smells particularly good after a shower of rain or on humid days when the scent drifts across the garden. It would make a lovely thicket in which to hide away. The leaves are good for picking during the summer and drying for pillows, sachets and pot-pourris.

FIXATIVES AND RESINOUS PERFUMES

Scent is volatile and will fade and disappear in time. A fixative helps to hold the scent for longer and often adds another element of scent of its own. There are many different fixatives of plant and animal origin. They are usually, but not necessarily, scented. Most were discovered long ago and have never been superseded, though there are chemical copies these days. It is a mystery how anyone discovered that the dried root of an inconspicuous iris or the scent glands of a civet had such a fixing property or, for that matter, that the strange substance called ambergris, produced in the intestines of a diseased sperm whale, gave up its perfume when dissolved in spirit and acted as a fixative for other scents.

Musk is obtained from the musk-deer, which lives in China, Assam and Tibet and it takes the animal four years to produce an ounce of musk. Civet came from the civet cat of Ethiopia, Thailand and Burma and was used extensively as a fixative in the sixteenth century. Rather thankfully, there are artificial appoximations of most of these animal-based fixatives but plant-based fixatives are still commonly used. Cedarwood and sandalwood fragrances are

This scented arbour has been built to cover a specially paved area big enough to take a garden seat and table. It is the sort of shady private place that makes a perfect retreat on a hot day.

109

used as fixatives in perfume-making, giving a warmth and staying power to other floral scents.

Resins, such as gum benjamin, are commonly available fixatives. Gum benjamin or benzoin is a hard, rocky resin. It is extracted from the styrax benzoin tree, which grows in Java, Thailand and Sumatra, by cutting the bark and collecting the liquid resin. It has only been commonly used since around the fifteenth century. The trees that produce the gum grow quickly and cuts are made in the bark when they are about seven years old. They exude the gum for another twelve years or so and are then cut down and renewed. Gum benzoin was once used in vast quantities to supply incense for the Russian Church. It has also been used as a burning medicine for the

Some of the strange and fascinating substances used as scent fixatives. Clockwise from top left: gum benzoin, musk crystals, orris root powder, myrrh grains and frankincense.

treatment of malaria. Whole pieces of gum benzoin are sometimes used in pot-pourris but it is often ground down to a coarse powder in a pestle and mortar. Tincture of benzoin, which is its liquid form, is often used as an astringent and preservative for cosmetics.

Tonquin beans are another useful, readily available fixative. They come from the Brazilian Amazon, and are borne on large tropical trees called *Dipterix odorata*. The large, shiny, black beans contain the substance coumarin, which is also found in new-mown hay, and have been used for centuries ground into sweet powders. Their scent increases as they age, and at one time they were used to perfume snuff. They are quite decorative left whole in pot-pourris as they have a shiny, blue-black skin with a slight bloom on it.

Frankincense and myrrh are two resinous perfumes that have been used for centuries. Around 2000 BC they were originally brought from the Yemen along a route known as the Incense Road, having been collected from trees growing in a small area at the southernmost tip of Arabia and on the coast of Somalia. The trees that produced the resin grew on rocky hillsides and difficult terrain, making the job of collecting and transporting it very hazardous. Frankincense came from the tree called *Boswellia serrata*, which has a smooth bark and fragrant leaves and wood. The bark was scored to release the sap, which was collected and dried. Myrrh was generally taken from the young shoots and stems of the shrubby bush *Commiphora myrrha* (*Balsamodendron myrrha*) but the very best resin came from the crushed, green berries. It would be possible to grow these two plants in cooler climates only in a hothouse. Frankincense has always been the most important ingredient for church incense, burnt alone or more usually mixed with benzoin and storax. If myrrh is added, the quantity is always half or less that of the frankincense. Such mixtures are based on Biblical formulas given by Moses for ceremonial rites. The word myrrh is derived from the Arabic word 'mur' meaning bitter and it was at one time used medicinally as well as for a perfume. It has antiseptic properties and is an excellent tonic and stimulant for diseased gums and as a mouthwash and tooth cleaner.

Storax is yet another natural perfume from a tree resin, this time from the tree *Liquidambar orientalis*. These days it is commonly sold as a liquid made by boiling the inner bark of the plant in sea water until the resin is released. It is aged for a long time before it develops its sweet balsam scent.

Patchouli leaves from the Indian tree *Pogostemon patchouli* are a useful, inexpensive natural fixative, although many people connect the scent with cheap perfumes and soaps with little subtlety. The trick is to combine the little, shiny, oval leaves with other things in the right proportions and not to let the patchouli fragrance dominate. For home-made pot-pourris, the simplest fixative to get hold of is probably orris root powder. It is interesting, however, to use a variety of materials. If you get more involved with home-made perfumes you may want to experiment with other things.

FINISHING THE
MOIST SUMMER POT-POURRI

By now you should have everything you need to finish off the summer pot-pourri (see pages 62-65). The rose petals will have had their long pickling in salt and should be brown and crumbly. The mixture remains leathery and a little damp but it should not be wet. The further flower additions you make are very much your decision and will depend on what other petals you have dried and what there is available from the garden or florist. The roses should remain the dominant part of the pot-pourri, both in fragrance and physical bulk, but other ingredients make a more interesting and subtle result. Any other flowers and leaves added to the moist pot-pourri should be completely dried, unlike the roses. Many flowers and leaves lose their scent once dried but some retain most or all of their scent. It is difficult to give amounts and proportions but by volume aim to add 1 part of other flowers to 5 parts of roses. To add colour and texture, but not necessarily scent, you could include some flowers and leaves from a much wider choice of ingredients. Any flower or leaf that dries and keeps its colour can be used.

SPICE AND FIXATIVE MIXTURE

To the mixture of rose petals, salt and other dried flowers you will now need to add spices and fixatives. The following recipe is based on traditional ones used in the eighteenth and nineteenth centuries when pot-pourri was made in this way. Make up a spice and fixative mixture in bulk and use what you need, then store the rest for another recipe. The same mixture can also be used for dry pot-pourri recipes. There are no strict rules about amounts of different ingredients so use your discretion as to how much spice mixture to add to flowers. As a rough guideline, use 1 cup or measure of spice and fixative mixture to 8 cups of completed rose and salt mixture.

INGREDIENTS

*125 grams (4½ ounces) ground
cloves*

*125 grams (4½ ounces) ground
cinnamon*

*125 grams (4½ ounces) ground
nutmeg*

*125 grams (4½ ounces) ground
allspice*

*125 grams (4½ ounces) ground
orris root*

*50 grams (1¾ ounces) brown
sugar*

*50 grams (1¾ ounces) ground
gum benzoin*

50 millilitres (¹⁄₁₀ pint) brandy

METHOD

Mix all the ingredients together. Once some of this spice mixture is thoroughly blended with the flowers you can then add a few extra whole spices and other things to create more visual interest and fragrance. Make a selection from the panel on page 113.

IDEAS FOR OTHER SCENTED INGREDIENTS

Rosemary leaves and flowers
Jasmine flowers
Lemon verbena leaves
Sweet woodruff leaves
Marjoram leaves and flowers
Lemon balm leaves
Mint leaves
Lavender
Scented geranium leaves
Sweet briar leaves
Bay leaves
Sage leaves
Myrtle leaves
Eucalyptus leaves
Green or purple basil leaves
Chamomile flower heads

INGREDIENTS TO ADD COLOUR AND TEXTURE

Tulip flowers
Pansy flowers
Violet leaves
Larkspur flowers
Peony flowers
Pot-marigold flowers
Hibiscus flowers
Delphinium flowers
Zinnia flowers
Rudbeckia flowers
Dahlia flowers
Lily flowers
Ranunculus flowers
Wallflower flowers
Love-in-a-mist flowers and
seed-heads
Celosia flowers
Fern leaves
Citrus leaves
Grasses
Tansy flowers
Hyssop flowers and leaves
Cornflower flowers

A mixture of extra dried flowers, leaves, whole and ground spices and fixatives to add to the moist pot-pourri.

Stir the whole thing with a wooden spoon or use your hands to combine everything thoroughly, making sure that the spices and fixatives are well distributed throughout the mixture. Put the pot-pourri into paper bags. Hide them away in a cool, dark place and forget about them for six weeks, except for giving them an occasional shake. After the curing time is up, put the pot-pourri into bowls and jars, preferably with a lid. Traditionally the lids were removed only when the pot was stood by a source of warmth so that the fragrance could be released.

ROSE AND GERANIUM MOIST POT-POURRI

This is a version of the previous recipe but with lots of scented geranium leaves and dried lavender added. A measure is based on a standard teacup.

INTERESTING
EXTRAS
Whole nutmegs
Short lengths of cinnamon
sticks
Whole mace
Juniper berries
Dried lemon- or orange-peel
Tonquin beans
Quassia chips
Cedarwood shavings
Whole cloves
Dried chillies
Whole allspice

INGREDIENTS *(continued overleaf)*

5 *measures rose petals and salt, already pickled and pressed*
2 *measures dried lavender flowers*
2 *measures scented geranium*

1 *measure oak moss*
½ *measure cinnamon sticks, roughly broken*
¼ *measure ground ginger*
½ *measure dried orange-peel, cut into small pieces*

113

leaves (ideally rose-scented
or lemon-scented)
1 measure spice and fixative
mixture (see page 112)

5 drops lavender essential oil
3 drops bergamot essential oil
4 drops rose geranium
essential oil

METHOD

In a large bowl, mix well together the rose petals and salt, lavender flowers and geranium leaves. Add the spice and fixative mixture then the oak moss, cinnamon, ginger and orange-peel. Finally add the essential oils, mix again and cure, using the method described for the moist summer pot-pourri (see page 65).

Even if scented geraniums did not have a ravishing range of scents they would be pretty enough to grow for their looks alone. The essential oil obtained from the rose-scented version and sold as rose geranium oil is a cheaper substitute for real rose oil.

DRY POT-POURRI FOR AUTUMN

This pot-pourri is full of the rich, autumnal colours of fruits, berries and seasonal flowers. The fragrance is orange-based, warm and inviting.

INGREDIENTS

2 cups dried pot-marigolds, whole or petals

1 cup dried rudbeckia, sunflowers or dahlias

1 cup dried rose hips

1 cup dried leaves such as bay, uva ursi, sage

½ cup dried orange-peel in large pieces

½ cup oak moss

½ cup cedarwood shavings

1 cup mixed dried chillies or small sweet peppers

¼ cup whole mace

1 cup spice and fixative mixture (see page 112)

3 drops petitgrain essential oil

3 drops orange or mandarin essential oil

4 drops cedarwood essential oil

METHOD

Mix all the dry ingredients together then add the spice and fixative mixture and mix again. Finally add the essential oil. Cure in paper bags for four to six weeks then bring out and display in large, shallow bowls and baskets or in a wooden tray or box. Decorate the top with whole, dried blooms of garden flowers, keeping the colour range to oranges, yellows and reds.

ROSE HIPS

When flowering is finished, some roses leave behind attractive rose hips, which are usually orange or bright red. Some roses have very small hips. As they are not fleshy they dry and preserve well and look good mixed into pot-pourri. Several of the species roses and climbers, such as *Rosa longicuspis*, have large clusters of these tiny hips. They should be picked before the first frosts cause them to wrinkle or split and then hung in bunches in a warm, airy room until they dry naturally. You can try drying some of the larger, more fleshy types of rose hip but some may rot or go mouldy before they are properly dried. The big, squashy hips from the Japanese *rugosa* roses are best left to decorate the garden and feed the birds into winter.

AUTUMN INDOOR GARDENING

As the autumn progresses, the weather turns cold and unfriendly. Outdoor gardening becomes less of a pleasure, but there is now time to think about growing scented plants indoors.

Indoor environments vary considerably. A large, airy house with big windows and good heating will offer a completely different

Left. *A conservatory provides an extra living room as well as a perfect place in which to grow plants, such as the scented jasmine climbing up and over the ceiling here. A room like this bridges the gap between seasons and can provide green leaves as well as scent all the year round.*

Above. *The thick, white petals of stephanotis look like they are carved from wax. The flowers are perfectly complemented by neat, glossy, dark-green foliage. Their longevity and exceptional fragrance made stephanotis the perfect flower for wiring into elaborate wedding bouquets and bridal decorations.*

home to plants from a cosy-roomed, small-windowed cottage with sneaky draughts around every door. Certain plants demand specific conditions while others are much more easygoing. A few indoor plants are designed for a short display and are not meant to be kept alive at all costs in the hope of them reflowering. Some have been forced, dwarfed or treated in ways to make them bloom well at the expense of the rest of the plant. Many indoor foliage plants come from tropical conditions of high humidity that are very difficult to re-create in a modern house.

The first step, then, is to decide which places in your home are suitable for certain plants and concentrate on these. Good light is vital for nearly every plant, which is why the windowsill is a popular resting place for so many potted plants. The windowsill can also mean unsuitable extremes of temperature, however. Winter nights can expose leaves to cold glass, freezing temperatures and cold draughts, while hot summer days can produce dazzling heat concentrated on the plant at midday. Move a table near to the window to get maximum light for the plants or choose windowsills carefully according to their position.

The Conservatory

Controlled conditions are possible indoors with a conservatory or heated greenhouse. One that opens off a living room is ideal as the plants can still be enjoyed at any time. These days conservatories are usually designed with people, rather than plants, in mind. They have become popular extensions to living space, so humidity controls and irrigation systems are rarely part of the design. To grow some wonderful, tender, scented plants, a proper old-fashioned conservatory would be ideal. There would be heat, good ventilation, shading where needed, a tiled floor on which to stand large containers and possibly soil beds too. Additionally, there could be wrought-iron plant display stands spilling with plants, twining climbers reaching up to the roof, hanging baskets and comfy wicker chairs.

A conservatory such as this would be a luxury indeed, along the lines of the Victorian conservatories that reached their peak of popularity in the nineteenth century. They were built to accommodate collections of rare and exotic plants and to provide delightful places in which to walk or drink tea. They also provided ideal venues for romantic assignations. Popular scented plants during this period included bouvardias, jasmine, daturas and mignonette. Scented geraniums, which require frost-free conditions, were favoured too.

The hoya is a wonderful scented plant for indoors that will particularly appreciate a greenhouse or conservatory. *Hoya bella* from India is a dwarf spreading plant ideal for a hanging basket. The fragrant, white, starry flowers have little purple centres. They grow in clusters, blooming from spring to autumn. *H. carnosa* is often called the wax plant. It climbs by use of aerial roots and can easily be trained into whichever direction you want it to grow. This time the little flowers are dusky pink but equally scented and they produce small droplets of fragrant nectar as the day goes by to attract insects to pollinate them. They demand high humidity in summer but can be kept cooler and drier during the winter.

Bouvardias have evergreen leaves and pretty, fragrant, tubular flowers. They require only a cool greenhouse and can be displayed in the house while they are flowering or stood outside for the warm summer months. Prune them hard each autumn to encourage growth of the new wood which carries the flowers. Because of the honey scent of their flowers, they were once popularly used for buttonholes and floral decorations. The white-flowered varieties seem to be the most highly scented.

Also suitable for the greenhouse and conservatory are *Stephanotis floribunda* and *Gardenia jasminoides*. Both have thick, dark-green evergreen leaves and white flowers with exotic scents. The stephanotis has long, twining stems, while the gardenia makes a shrub rather like a camellia. Stephanotis has thick, waxy flowers, which last well and have made it a very popular flower to use for elaborate, formal wedding bouquets and headdresses. The plant needs plenty of warmth and light in summer and supports for it to twine around. It comes from Madagascar where it is known as the Madagascar jasmine. Its scent is wonderful but can become almost overpowering in a small space.

Gardenias are delicate flowers with the texture of fine suede or unglazed porcelain. They bruise easily and are spoilt if handled. Their scent is similar to orange blossom and during the 1930s they were incredibly popular as a buttonhole flower for evening wear. There are many different species but *jasminoides* is the one commonly sold as a pot plant. The double version, 'Florida Plena' is particularly strongly scented. They must be kept at least at 13°C (55°F) during winter and need plenty of soft water during spring. Some people find them difficult to grow. The blooms often fall off at the bud stage, but given the right conditions they are spectacular. They make a very pretty standard shrub by pruning and training from a single straight stem.

A different kind of plant that can live in a conservatory or be grown indoors from a tuberous root is *Polianthes tuberosa*. A native of Mexico, it produces a spike of highly scented flowers, some say the most highly scented of all. The flowers are white and star-shaped and were used at one time to produce the popular tuberose perfume. Like dahlias, they can be grown outdoors if the tubers are lifted and dried off in the autumn, but they are probably easier to cultivate as an indoor plant. *Polianthes tuberosa* was used for bridal bouquets at one time, but now seems to have lost favour.

During the autumn months there are fewer scented flowers growing in the garden to pick and bring indoors. There may be some late roses and nicotiana. To add to these, make use of foliage such as glossy myrtle and enjoy its spicy fragrance, which is released when the plant is handled.

Winter
Scented Memories

Cold, crisp air keeps scent at bay and most plants dormant. But a few, very special plants choose to flower now and are all the more welcome. Cut and taken indoors, their fragrance is released more strongly and combines with the spicy scents of winter and the perfumed results of summer harvesting.

If you know what to plant it is still perfectly possible to have scented flowers during the bleakest months. This is the evergreen shrub Mahonia × media *'Charity'*.

People new to gardening are always surprised by the winter garden. Far from being bleak and colourless, the garden can be filled with a wide variety of blooms at this time of the year. And winter is a particularly good time for fragrant flowers. Many are subtle and certainly not spectacular but they make up for any deficiency in size and colour by their quite magnificent scents. As these plants flower during some of the coldest months of the year, the blossoms are wonderfully long lasting on the branch, an added bonus to the fact that they are blooming at all when so much else is lying dormant or underground.

Many gardeners come slowly to winter gardening. In their early gardening years they are seduced by the colour and abundance of the hectic summer months and ignore the rest of the year. Often, though, the discreet charms of the winter flowerers catch up with most of them after a few seasons and they are smitten, eventually declaring that these are the months they prefer in the garden. With the bare outlines and architecture of the place in proper evidence and just a few beautiful scented plants to remind one that spring is never far away, the winter garden has a special attraction.

WINTER-FLOWERING SHRUBS

Many of the shrubs that flower in winter do so on bare branches followed by not very attractive leaves. It is sensible, therefore, to plan quite carefully where these winter plants are to go. They should be near to the house so that you get some benefit from them by looking at and sniffing them occasionally. You will not be able to do this if they are tucked away up a long muddy path or hidden around a corner. One or two shrubs are sufficiently pretty and noticeable from a distance to be planted and seen from the house. It is also a good idea to site them more or less together rather than dotting them about among other things. If you have the perfect space in the right part of the garden it is pleasing to make a small winter area. This would not only include flowering shrubs and trees but there might also be winter bulbs beneath them, flowering winter iris perhaps, some good foliage and other plants grown for their winter bark, good colour or shapely silhouettes.

There are few scented flowering winter evergreens, but there is one excellent plant that suits many different gardens. Sarcococca never grows too big but remains a neat, bushy, little evergreen. Its small, pointed, unscented leaves resemble myrtle foliage, even though it comes from the same family as box. During the winter, tiny, brownish-white flowers bloom all the way up the stems between the leaf axils. It can be planted on its own or in a group to make a low edging or small hedge at the front of a border or beside a path. Sarcococcas are happy growing in shade. They are natives of the area from the Himalayas to southern China and throughout south-east Asia. They are hardy and easygoing and, having reached a certain size, seem to stay put, which is excellent when you have little space. The two varieties most commonly available are *Sarcococca hookeriana* and *S. humilis*, both reaching around 90 centimetres (3 feet) to 1 metre (3⅓ feet) and having a rich, fruity scent.

The *Daphne* genus includes around 400 different types of evergreen and deciduous shrubs. Several of them are winter-flowering, carrying their beautifully scented flowers on bare stems. Daphnes are neat and slow growing, generally needing little pruning or control, although they do have a reputation for sometimes being tricky to cultivate or dying suddenly with no apparent cause. They prefer an alkaline to an acid soil and can be propagated by cuttings or by layering branches down into the soil.

The best winter-flowering daphne is *Daphne mezereum*, which is very hardy and native to southern European woodlands. It is an

The flowers of Hamamelis mollis *appear in small clusters of tiny petals like tattered strips of bright-yellow paper on the bare stems. The honey scent is strong and far-reaching but do not cut branches for indoors as the plant is very slow-growing.*

Above. *The daphne is a family of shrubs with a wide choice of scented varieties. There are several winter-flowering ones like this* D. odora alba.

Right. Daphne mezereum *is very showy for a winter-flowering shrub. The pink or purple flowers bloom on bare branches and are a definite benefit when there are few other flowers in the garden. After the flowers will come bright-orange berries.*

upright plant that grows only about 3 centimetres (1¼ inch) a year and needs a cool, moist soil for its roots to grow in. Its flowers are a deep purplish-pink and look wonderfully exotic smothering the pale-brown stems. There is also a pure-white-flowered version, which blooms later in the year. The flowers curl back to reveal bright-orange stamens inside the bloom, which have a sweet, heady perfume. Daphnes resent being pruned or having their stems cut so resist the temptation to pick little twigs for the house. The flowers are followed by bright berries later, which often drop and seed themselves around the parent plant. *D. mezereum* is in fact one daphne best grown from seed, even though it takes up to two years to germinate.

Another evergreen winter daphne that is a good choice for a fragrant garden is *Daphne odora* from China. The form 'Aureo-marginata' is better, however, as it is hardier than the type and the cream-edged leaves are more interesting when the shrub is not in bloom. It flowers from mid-winter through to early spring and the scent from the clusters of pink, tubular flowers carries on the still air. Its strong fragrance has an undertone of spice. The shrub grows to a dense, rounded bush never more than about 90 centimetres (3 feet) tall. Plant it in a sheltered position as it does not enjoy the buffeting of icy winds, which can burn the leaves and flowers.

The *Lonicera* or honeysuckle genus includes many non-climbing, shrubby plants that few people know about. Most have wonderfully scented flowers, just as the climbing ones do, though the shrubby version's flowers are usually quite small and insignificant but unmistakably those of a honeysuckle. Some are semi-evergreen. This means that they are largely deciduous but a few leaves remain on the branches right through the winter. The foliage on these shrubs is generally rather boring with quite large oval leaves of a dull mid-green. Although not a plant to make a feature of during the summer months, it is completely transformed in mid-winter when the flowers are blooming all over it.

Look out for the species *Lonicera fragrantissima* and the hybrid *L. × purpusii*. The latter is a hybrid between the first and *L. standishii*, both of which are Chinese species. It has barer branches when it flowers than *fragrantissima*, which is semi-evergreen. The creamy-white flowers of both kinds are produced back to back along the branches and the fragrance is sweet, similar to a climbing honeysuckle scent but with a lemony undertone. It is one of the strongest scents in the winter garden, carrying long distances on still days. A twig or two brought indoors is a real treat during winter as they fill the house with a summery fragrance. The shrubby honeysuckles make quite large and not particularly elegant shrubs but they can be kept pruned and within bounds. A certain amount of old wood cut away encourages new growth and the flowers seem to bloom happily on both old and new wood.

Yet another winter-flowering shrub with a delicious scent is wintersweet *Chimonanthus fragrans*, a member of the allspice family and related to the Carolina allspice. It has strange, waxy, almost transparent, bell-shaped flowers with pointed ends to the petals. They cluster close against the bare stems, growing from the axils of the old leaves, and are hardly noticeable at first. If you stop and look up into the yellowish flowers made up partly of eight outer petals you can see also six inner brownish-red petals. The scent is lovely, a mixture of the scents of jonquil and violet, and it carries well over a distance of 40 metres (130 feet) or so. The shrub can grow up to 3 metres (10 feet) tall. It is often grown against a wall, although it is fine in a sheltered position anywhere in the garden. After flowering, the large, pointed, pale-green leaves are produced. Give wintersweet good, rich, moist soil and a sunny position if possible. The garden writer Margery Fish describes picking sprays of the

Lonicera fragrantissima *is one of the winter-flowering honeysuckles. It never fails to produce hundreds of cream, fragrant flowers over a long period of time and is excellent picked and brought indoors.*

shrub along with other little winter-garden treasures to decorate her dining room and their scent filling the house for days. Although the flowers are often in bloom during hard weather and severe frosts, they seem to recover quickly from the frozen state. The flowers appear in waves to replace each other as they fade naturally.

Witch hazel is another winter-flowerer. It is both decorative and scented. Although a slow grower, it can eventually make a large shrub or small tree given good conditions. There are several species in the family but the commonly grown winter-flowering type is *Hamamelis mollis* from China. The flowers are curious, made up of masses of narrow, twisted strips of petals growing straight from the branch. A bright, golden-yellow variety is most often seen but there are paler and rusty-red versions too. Witch hazel prefers slightly acid to alkaline soil and is happy in light shade. The large, coarse leaves appear after flowering and have wonderful autumn colouring. The scent is strong and delicious with a hint of incense to it. A large shrub of witch hazel can look quite breathtaking in full bloom on a sunny winter day with the light streaming through the petals from behind. Plant it so it can be seen from the house and give it a dark background to throw the flowers into relief.

Another yellow-flowered, scented shrub is mahonia. There are 70 species in the genus but one of the best for its winter scent is *Mahonia japonica*, a native of Japan. It is an extremely tough and hardy evergreen shrub with spiky leaves. The lemon-yellow flowers grow from the base of the leaf shoots in long plumes known as racemes, which are in groups of about eight, making a bouquet of the sweetly scented blossoms. The flower stems are quite long and can be picked individually for flower arrangements. The shrub can be in flower for several weeks through the winter and it is very attractive to early insects. Once pollinated, the flowers turn into elegant, blue-green berries which have a soft, grey bloom on them. The whole plant has a dramatic look suitable for small town gardens where good outlines and definite shapes are needed. It is happy in partial shade but likes a moist soil.

EVERGREEN FOLIAGE SCENTS

Many evergreen and coniferous trees have scented foliage all year round. Often used as background plants, windbreak, or hedges, they nevertheless have distinctive scents that carry on the air or are released when the tree is brushed against.

Thuya plicata has a lovely scent of ripe apples from its small, scaly leaves. Native species of thuya can reach immense sizes in the wild, but for gardens, there are many small and slow-growing types to choose from. They all tend towards a conical habit of growth but can be cut as a hedge better than is the case with many conifers.

Junipers are part of the huge cypress family and the genus of 60 or so species have pungent scented foliage. There are tall, columnar ones to choose from and many dwarf or prostrate forms for gardens. Some varieties have highly scented wood, which used to be burned indoors for its scent and once flavoured smoked hams in Scotland. Forks and spoons were also carved from it and retained a slight perfume all their life. The small, fragrant blue-black berries have traditionally been used to season game and pork and to flavour gin. The foliage has a powerfully resinous smell. In the sixteenth century branches of it were cut to make arbours or bowers to sit in. The scent was supposed to invigorate whoever sat beneath them. An essential oil is obtained from the berries for use in perfumes.

Juniperus hibernica is probably one of the most well-known junipers. The tall, narrow Irish juniper has glaucous foliage and the

During winter we often pick traditionally festive evergreens to bring indoors but rarely use some of the many other types, such as cypress and thuja, which have lovely aromatic or resinous scents. Most evergreens have either healthy, glossy foliage or ferny leaves in shades of grey and blue-green which are very decorative. Try mixing several kinds together.

wood when cut is a startling yellow and very fragrant. *Juniperus virginiana* is the red 'cedar' used for many commercial purposes including providing wood for the manufacture of pencils and the extraction of 'cedar' oil.

Pine cones from trees in the genus *Pinus* have been used over the centuries for flavouring and scenting all manner of things and the little seeds inside were used as food. In Italy the cones used to be placed in wine vats to infuse into the grape juice while it was fermenting. Dried cones were put among clothes to scent them or hung on strings around a room to give the air the smell of a pine forest. They were originally called pine-nuts or pine-apples until the tropical fruit of that name appeared in northern Europe. The Scots pine *Pinus sylvestris* was used to make turpentine, pitch and tar from its bark and the good, waterproof wood was used for boat building. Trees from the genus *Picea* (spruce) are also scented and resinous as

Right. *The flowers bloom in delicate clusters at the end of the long stems. The scent is heavy and can be almost overpowering in a confined space.*

Below. *'Paper white' narcissi shoot up from their container with alarming speed and strength. Before flowering they often need to be supported with twiggy sticks or small canes.*

anyone knows who has brought a Norway spruce indoors to celebrate Christmas. There are many garden trees to choose from in this group, including weeping varieties and blue-foliaged kinds. Most of them grow into large trees in time so they are only suitable if you have plenty of space.

Eucalyptuses are in the myrtle family. Some types are evergreen, others deciduous. They are natives of Australia, where their common name gum tree, describes the sticky, balsamic gum that exudes from the trunk of some varieties. Eucalyptus oil is extracted from the twigs and leaves. The oil is powerfully antiseptic and was discovered to be useful as late as 1788, when it was distilled by two doctors who used it to treat chest and lung conditions. There are only a few varieties that are hardy enough for colder climates but it is a lovely garden plant, adding an unexpected grey-blue foliage colour among the usual yellowish greens. Although they grow very quickly, eucalyptus trees can be kept to shrub size by cutting back the branches regularly. Flower-arrangers adore the leaves and the foliage is also useful dried as it keeps its distinctive eucalyptus perfume. One of the commonest and hardiest types to be grown in gardens is *Eucalyptus gunnii*, a native of Tasmania.

Another shrub with evergreen, aromatic foliage is the bright, glossy-leaved *Choisya ternata* or Mexican orange blossom. This makes a good-tempered, easy shrub, which has scented flowers through the year, often in two crops. If pressed, the leaves give out an astringent, orangey scent from the essential oils contained within them. It is a first-class garden plant that is perfectly happy to be quite severely pruned and stays bright and glossy through the winter. In very cold or exposed gardens it should be protected by a wall or be planted up against the house in case icy winds clip the foliage. It can grow into a rounded bush up to about 3 metres (10 feet) in height but it can be kept much smaller than this and does not seem to object to drastic or regular pruning.

THE QUICKEST SCENTED BULBS

If you have not yet managed to plant winter-flowering bulbs and feel starved of fresh flowers and scent, there is a way to rectify this. 'Paper White' is a bunch-flowered narcissus that is ideal for last-minute winter planting, taking around eight weeks to flower. These bulbs do not even need all the paraphernalia of soil and proper garden pots as they are equally happy grown on pebbles or in sand. This means that any kind of waterproof container can be put to use as a temporary home for them. Make sure, though, that there is room for all the bulbs to fit without touching each other and that there is some depth for the roots to grow down and develop. Plant at least six bulbs at a time so that there is plenty of bloom. They tend to zoom upwards, making great, long stems and therefore need plenty of the flowers at the top to make them look balanced. Baskets of these narcissi are popular Christmas decorations in the USA. They are a mixture of wintriness and exuberance that makes them look very festive. For a natural look, the tops of the bulbs can be covered in a layer of moss if they are blooming at any time during the winter or spring. You could go a little wilder for a Christmas display and use crumpled cellophane or shiny ribbon bows piled on the surface.

'Paper Whites', as the name suggests, is a pure-white narcissus. If you prefer more colour, choose the golden-yellow variety 'Grand Soleil d'Or'. Another white version, 'Chagford', has a scarlet-orange centre to each flower. To plant them, put a layer of washed pebbles, grit or chippings to within 5 centimetres (2 inches) of the top of the container you are using and tuck in a small piece of char-coal. Sit the bulbs on top of this. Pile more pebbles around the bulbs so they are anchored in place. Pour in water, preferably rainwater, to just below the base of the bulbs. This is easier to see if you have planted into a clear-glass container. Put the bowl away in a very cool place – dark or light – and leave it for about five weeks. The roots will have grown and the shoots will be showing well. Bring the bowl out into a slightly warmer temperature of around 10° C (50° F) in light, airy conditions. As the plants develop they can be given slightly more warmth but if forced too soon they will get too tall and leggy. Even if you keep the plants at an ideal temperature you may still need to support the tall leaves and stems. Use thin sticks or canes or make a circle of wire on a stick to stop them flopping over.

If you feel like trying something more complicated you could plant the bulbs into soil and, when they are ready to come out from their five weeks of cold, repot them into a container with some small-leaved ivies. These can then be trained up sticks or into a shape made from wire to make a background for the white flowers.

HOUSE SCENTS AND CULINARY FRAGRANCE

Certain scents please everyone: wood from fruit trees burning in an open fireplace, a bowl of home-grown fruit in a sunny window or the spicy smell of baking finding its way upstairs from the kitchen. Many of these kinds of scents are rare these days and therefore all the more welcome. In our well-heated and well-sealed houses the good smells can linger but so can the bad, usually combining in the end to make the special scent that spells home. In the days of less efficient ways of cleaning clothes, bedding and bodies, much time and trouble was spent trying to rid a house of bad odours and to import better ones to mask them. The strewing of herbs, rushes and foliage on floors was partly to blot up the spills from open cooking pots and careless eaters and to make a beaten earth floor more pleasant to live with, but also to add their own fragrance. Sweet rushes, leafy herbs and other special plants were used to freshen the air. The popularity of flowers and herbs, such as lavender and small pots of growing rosemary and mint, was much to do with adding a fresh scent to musty, stale, unaired rooms. Scented plants were stood in window-sills so that the movement of air swept the sweet scents inside and many leaves and flowers were believed to repel insects and vermin too. Our habit of cutting and arranging flowers in vases and containers to decorate rooms must, in part, be related to the old customs of bringing flowers and herbs inside for practical reasons.

Introducing scents into the house is difficult to get right. Aggressive and unnatural air-fresheners and pot-pourris are often unpleasant if too strong or sometimes downright disgusting mixed with smells that are already around. There are several less drastic methods of improving the ambience of a house than resorting to a spray can of chemicals, all of which are more subtle, natural and usually cheaper than factory-made fragrances. Herbs or spices added to a pan of boiling water can do wonders for stale air and smells. Try a bunch of rosemary or mint in the summer or a spice mix of cinnamon bark and orange peel in winter. Just toss whatever you choose into the pan of water and let it bubble away. Leave internal doors open to allow the scent to move around the house.

Essential oil can be used in every room to great effect. You can buy special fragrance rings that sit around a light fitting. A few drops of oil are added and the warmth from the bulb causes the oil to evaporate, releasing its scent gently over several hours. To begin with keep to fresh, outdoor smells rather than heavy, exotic scents. Find out which scents you prefer or make blends with several different fragrances. A hot bath run with fresh herbs, a few drops of essential oils or a home-made, scented bath-bag will scent the room for quite a long time after you have finished bathing.

Keep cupboards and closed storage spaces fresh with scented powders or tuck small pieces of cotton wool impregnated with essential oils into little fabric or paper bags to hang in a corner of the cupboard or on the back of a door. Another idea is to drop the oil on to strips of cotton tape or ribbon and tie these to clothes hangers or pin them into cupboard frames. Choose a traditional perfume, such as cedarwood or sandalwood, and include one or more of the moth repellents, thyme, southernwood and lavender.

If you grow and harvest your own herbs during the summer months do not discard all the old stems from which you have stripped the leaves. Keep them dried and in small bundles and burn them on an open coal or wood fire. Lavender stems smell particularly good. Make bundles of cinnamon sticks too but do not burn them; simply leave them in a warm place, such as beside the fire or on a warm radiator.

Make pretend pomanders with whole spices such as cloves, allspice and star anise. Glue the spices using a glue gun and stick them all over small, floral, foam balls until they are densely covered and look rather like traditional clove and citrus pomanders. Pile these spice balls into bowls and stand them in a warm place where the scent will be obvious.

Fragrant cheer

Cheering winter brews rely as much on smell as taste to do their comforting work. All the old punches and neguses were heavily spiced and fragrant with citrus peels, nutmeg and cloves. A little thought along these lines can turn mundane hot chocolate into a cinnamon-scented delight and plain cider into a spicy, warming drink.

SPICED WINTER CIDER
This makes enough for four servings.

INGREDIENTS

600 millilitres (1¼ pints) still dry cider
150 millilitres (⅓ pint) fresh orange juice
50 grams (1¾ ounces) demerara sugar

2 strips orange-peel
2 cinnamon sticks
10 whole cloves
1 teaspoon freshly grated nutmeg
1 red apple, sliced and cored

METHOD

In a large, non-reactive pan heat the cider with the orange juice, peel, sugar and spices, stirring well. Bring just to the boil and simmer for about four minutes. Do not let it boil furiously. Strain the liquid into a big bowl, add the apple rings and serve into mugs. A measure of rum can be added just before serving if you like.

CINNAMON HOT CHOCOLATE
This makes enough for two servings.

INGREDIENTS

300 millilitres (½ pint) milk
2 teaspoons unsweetened cocoa powder

1 teaspoon sugar or to taste
½ teaspoon ground cinnamon cinnamon sticks

METHOD

Warm the milk in a non-stick saucepan. Sprinkle on the cocoa, sugar and cinnamon and stir and whisk the chocolate mixture while it heats gently. Take if off the heat just before it boils. Pour into cups and give each serving a cinnamon stick to stir it with. For a luxurious drink, top with unsweetened whipped cream and dust the surface with freshly grated nutmeg and a pinch more cinnamon.

The pleasures of mulled wine drunk on a cold night are as much to do with the scent of the drink as its taste. Few people can resist a glass of red wine warmed with wintery spices such as cloves and cinnamon, and enlivened by citrus fruit zest.

FRUITS, POMANDERS, BEADS AND SPICES

The fresh fruits of winter were always doubly precious years ago when people mostly had to make do with what was grown locally and carefully stored during the months of scarcity. The tree fruits such as apples, pears and quinces all store satisfactorily, in some case for several weeks or even months. The scent of an apple storeroom is delicious and distinctive, unknown to most of us now that our fruit comes cold and perfect from special high-tech storage warehouses. Citrus fruits seem to survive modern processing a little better. They still yield up their delicious scent when the peel is punctured or scraped, releasing a little puff of citrus oil into the surrounding air. The zest or finely grated peel of orange and lemon is still a magical ingredient for all kinds of foods but be sure to buy organically grown or at least untreated and unwaxed fruits if you intend to use the peel fresh in food.

Most of us are familiar with clove and orange pomanders cured in a mixture of spices and used nowadays as a decoration or quaint reminder of days past. The first pomanders, however, were not made from fruit in this way. In fact they were small caskets or round boxes containing little pieces of rare and scented resins. Some of these containers were exquisitely beautiful in their own right, like elaborate and decorative pieces of jewellery. The word pomander is thought to be a corruption of *pomme d'ambre* or 'apple of amber', suggesting that the earliest ones were round and apple-shaped. Suspended on chains, they were carried in the belief that they warded off foul odours and infectious diseases, especially the plague. Henry V of England carried with him a 'musk ball of gold', probably a trophy from his French campaigns. Illnesses were believed to be carried on the air and in bad smells so the little pomanders were sniffed at in the same way that small herbal nosegays were used where many people gathered together, particularly in public places such as courtrooms.

There were also pomanders that looked like large beads made from mixtures of gum and resin or fixative scents. They were sometimes strung together and worn as necklaces or bracelets. Elizabeth I of England carried a simple ball pomander made from ambergris and benzoin. A more elaborate type was made with several sections, just like the segments of an orange, which hinged open from the base of a central core. When the segments were closed against the core they were locked at the top with a ring. Each segment had a flap that slid back to allow it to be filled with perfume so different scents could be carried at the same time.

Other devices were invented and used over the centuries to carry and diffuse perfumes. A cassolette or printanier was a little box made from gold, silver or ivory with a perforated lid. Into this was put a highly scented paste made from animal fixatives, such as civet and ambergris, spices and citrus oils. It was meant for personal use and the scent was inhaled whenever it was felt necessary.

Apples and oranges stuck with cloves provided a cheap and simple alternative to the more elaborate and precious pomanders. Versions of this idea are really the only kind of thing we make these days along the same lines. You can use any citrus fruit – lime, orange or lemon – though a round shape is the most usual choice. Stud the fruit all over with whole cloves, chosen for their large size and perfect formation. Make a hole with a knitting needle or sharp wooden skewer first as the clove stalk is not usually sharp enough to pierce the peel. Either work all over the surface neatly in bands, in a spiral or completely randomly, whichever you prefer. Leave a strip of peel uncovered right around the fruit if you intend to tie a ribbon or tape around it with which to hang it up later. Spiking fruit with cloves is quite a fiddly, sticky task. Give yourself plenty of time to tackle it at a leisurely pace. The cloves should be quite close together as you work across the peel but remember that they will get even closer as the fruit shrinks while curing. Finally, put the pomander in a bag with some of the curing spice mixture (see recipe on page 112) and shake it well. Leave it in the mixture for a few days then take it out, brush off any excess powder and put the pomander somewhere dry and cool to continue curing. This may take several weeks. When it has shrunk and is hard and cured, attach a ribbon or tape and use it.

In the sixteenth century all kinds of different methods were devised for perfuming things. The roots of plants such as ploughman's spikenard *Inula conyza* were burnt to scent a house. In Scotland, lengths of pine root were set to burn slowly like a candle to fill a room with the resinous, clean smell of pine. Another burning root came from elecampane, a wild flower growing commonly by roadsides that produced an aroma of violets when it smouldered. Seeds, too, were used for their scenting properties. One of the most popular came from the angelica herb *Angelica officinalis*. A handful of the dry seeds were thrown into a frying pan and toasted over a fire. If you grow the lovely tall and stately angelica in your garden this might be worth trying. Angelica essential oil obtained from the seeds of the plant is one of the herb flavourings used in the liqueur made by the monks of La Grande Chartreuse.

Clothes, especially gloves, were often scented before being worn. This was done by a combination of methods. Bags of sweet powders were stored with the clothes and the fabric was sprinkled with perfumed waters. Closets and chests were made from scented woods such as juniper and sandalwood and there were elaborate ways to cure leather for clothes that gave it a permanent perfume for the rest of its life as a garment.

The curious blackish-red beads are made from rose petals. To make them prettier they have been strung between wooden beads on a cherry-red cord to wear as a necklace. The warmth of the skin releases the rose scent.

SPICE BEADS

This recipe is probably quite close to the original ones for wax and resin beads but it is made from ingredients that are easily available today.

INGREDIENTS

125 grams (4½ ounces) powdered gum tragacanth	60 grams (2 ounces) powdered orris root
125 grams (4½ ounces) gum benzoin	60 grams (2 ounces) powdered nutmeg
60 grams (2 ounces) cinnamon	glycerine
	essential oil of your choice

METHOD

Mix all the dry ingredients together well. Add some glycerine, drop by drop, and mix well. When you have a stiff paste add several drops of an essential oil to perfume the beads. You could choose a rose or rose geranium oil or a blend of your choice. Then roll the paste into little beads and put them to dry on a piece of non-stick parchment. When they are semi-dry, push a needle through each one to make a hole for the thread. Thread on to a cord when they are dry. When the beads begin to lose their perfume add a few more drops of essential oil to each one.

Another way to make beads is to use paper mâché. For something as small and fine as beads it is better to use tissue paper or something less coarse than the usual newspaper. Cellulose wallpaper paste is generally used as the glue these days or you can make an old-fashioned flour-and-water paste if you prefer. There are several ways of adding scent to the beads. You can use rose water or orange flower water when making up the wallpaper paste. Drops of essential oil can be applied to the beads as you layer the strips or pieces of paper or you can simply apply a few drops when the beads are complete or even dried. Experiment to see what gives the best results. You can simply roll small balls of shredded paper into rough beads or any shape you want, or build up layers of small strips, creating shapes more slowly. To finish, use a water-based paint that allows the scent to escape from the paper but ensure that it is not liable to stain clothes or come off should it get wet by mistake. You could experiment with transparent coloured inks to colour the beads instead of an opaque paint. If you are good at making things you will probably be able to create all kinds of jewellery, such as earrings and bracelets, as well as the simple strings of beads.

UNWANTED GUESTS

Scent has been the answer to repelling all kinds of unwanted household guests for centuries. Over the years the best herbs and fragrances for the job have been discovered and perfected. We are less likely these days, fortunately, to have some of the most unpleasant visitors and vermin that medieval houses might have harboured but we all suffer from flying pests invading the house during the summer or a sudden line of ants appearing and heading for the food storage. A bad infestation of pests may need immediate and serious action but herbal and fragrant solutions are sometimes an efficient and simple preventative for a small irritation.

Certain fragrant herbs have always been known for their protective qualities and used in several different forms. Many of the mints are reputedly good at repelling flies and other flying insects and have been used in simple ways such as hanging a bunch of the fresh leaves just inside an open window on summer days. A jug or vase of mint stems can be stood on a windowsill and will last longer than a hanging bunch if the stems are in water. Planting mint outside a kitchen door or window is doubly useful for adding to the cooking pot and salads and to see off flies. Peppermint is claimed to be obnoxious to mice so that a few drops of peppermint essential oil in attics and cellars and places where they may come in to nest would seem to be a good preventative measure.

Pomanders made from oranges and cloves (see page 134) hanging in a room are supposed to keep flies away. An elder tree planted by a kitchen door is supposed to have the same effect, though it is doubtful whether many people would like the rank smell of the plant so close to the house. Other old-fashioned remedies for warding off flies include boiling quassia chips in water and putting the resultant liquid in a saucer sweetened with sugar. This is apparently harmless to humans but lethal to flies. A less unpleasant method involves leaving a sponge soaked in water and oil of lavender in a room. The sponge is moistened with boiling water twice a day and the oil replaced only once a week. Whether this repels flies or not it is nevertheless a pleasant scent to have in any room.

Oil of citronella is a well-known treatment to protect human flesh from midge and mosquito bites, which can be so bad at times in the summer that you are driven indoors on warm evenings. The citrus scent is a bit overpowering so you could try a solution of quassia chips simmered in water in the proportions of 4 tablespoons of quassia wood chips to 600 millilitres (1¼ pints) of water. Leave the infusion to cool down then strain it and dab the liquid on to exposed areas of skin before venturing out.

Dogs and cats also commonly suffer from insect bites. Pennyroyal *Mentha pulegium*, a diminutive member of the mint family, is supposed to be intolerable to fleas. Rub your pet's coat with the green herb and tuck small pieces into its bedding. Pennyroyal acquired its name because it was originally used in royal households when fleas were an ubiquitous irritation and happy to feed on peasants or kings. This little plant loves to grow in moist situations and has a very pungent, strong camphor perfume.

The clothes moth is nowhere near the problem to households that it once was. In the days when woollen and silk clothes could not be dry-cleaned or washed in water they were often stored in cupboards in a less than clean state and were wonderfully inviting to the grubs of any moths that fed on fabrics. All kinds of remedies were tried to prevent an infestation and certain herbs were chosen as the most effective. Now that we keep clothes clean there is not such a problem, though people who live in the country still find the occasional hopeful moth. To be doubly sure, hang sachets and sweet bags among clothes and include little bundles of specific herbs to help protect precious stored garments.

The classic closet herbs are southernwood, tansy, santolina and lavender. Lad's love or southernwood *Artemisia abrotanum* has pinnate, greyish leaves. Its scent is pungent and lemony with a

Just a few of the classic closet herbs used at one time to repel insects and vermin. Pick them fresh and make small bunches to dry and hang where you need them. Included here are santolina, southernwood, hyssop, lavender and marjoram.

strong, savoury, and sometimes unpleasant undertone. Known in France as garde-robe it has always been used to deter moths and can be dried to crumble with other herbs into sachets or just hung in small bunches to dry in the cupboard or drawer. Tansy *Tanacetum vulgare* is a wayside flower best not brought into the herb garden as it runs through flower beds and romps around the whole garden in no time. It has tall stems with little, hard, button-yellow flowers with a sharp, acrid scent. The whole plant dries very well, keeping its colour and scent. Santolina or cotton lavender *Santolina chamaecyparissus* has silver-grey foliage reminiscent of the structure of coral. It is a good-natured plant, excellent grown as a border or edging to a herb garden and it can be severely pruned into strict shapes. The dried aromatic leaves are traditionally part of the moth deterrent used in old-fashioned households and it is still a good pot-pourri and sweet-bag ingredient. Lavender has been well covered already but it is a useful scent to mix with the more powerful and pungent insect repellents as it is one of the few that can hold its own with such strong fragrances.

At one time, chests and furniture used for storage of clothes and linens were made from or lined with cedar wood, juniper or sandalwood. Copy this idea by impregnating wood curls or shavings with a wood essential oil. Cedar is delicious, juniper a little fresher, while sandalwood is definitely heavier and more exotic. Tie the shavings inside a fabric bag or just a strong paper bag and hang it in among clothes in the cupboard. Never let anything impregnated with essential oil directly touch fabrics in case it stains or marks them.

WINTER POT-POURRIS

Winter is an excellent time to make special scented mixtures from your store of dried summer ingredients. You can choose to make essentially decorative pot-pourris, which happen to smell good as well, or you can get creative with the fragrance and build mixtures around a scented theme. Winter suggests the need for warm, spicy scents and deep, rich colours but the shock of bright, startling colours is welcome too during long, grey days. Pot-pourris do not have to be subtle and delicate; they can be bright and chunky and full of wonderful textural ingredients. Displayed in colourful, clashing bowls or boxes they immediately lose their fusty, musty, old-fashioned image. Bright-coloured mixtures look good in papier mâché containers or stained wood. Glass and china are never very sympathetic as a background to the papery, dried textures of flowers and other ingredients. Baskets are a ubiquitous choice for the display of pot-pourri as they always look good, though they are not particularly practical when used to hold a fine or powdery mixture. Line any very open-weave baskets with a layer of paper before piling in the pot-pourri. Lidded containers are excellent as they can be kept closed most of the time to preserve the scent and colour except when you want to enjoy the pot-pourri. Nearly all dried flowers will eventually fade, usually due to strong light bleaching out the colours. Try not to stand pot-pourris in places, such as a windowsill, which receive direct sunlight, even for short periods of time. Keep them further inside a room if possible.

If you intend making several different mixtures from your stored ingredients, work methodically and make a small sample mix combining the ingredients you hope to use. You could put a little of every ingredient on to a large tray and see how they look together. Use colourful picture references from magazines, scraps of paper or favourite fabric designs and try to create a pot-pourri to match. Remember that some ingredients are heavier than others and often drop down through pot-pourri mixtures to disappear at the bottom of the container. Small, round berries and spices have a habit of doing this, unless you display everything in a very shallow bowl with ingredients only one layer deep.

Mixtures based around shades and tones of one colour, or a mixture of only two colours, often look better than random colour mixtures, though the old-fashioned, cottage-garden jumble of every colour under the sun can look good too. A lot will depend on the ingredients you can get hold of or have grown specially. If you plan to use roses as the main ingredient, sticking to one or two colours creates a good effect. You could base a mixture on deep-red and purplish-black rose petals, adding sharp accents of scarlet and crimson with berries, spices, chillies and other flower-heads and petals. If you have dried or bought roses as complete flower-heads then leave most of them whole if you want a good, strong-looking pot-pourri with texture and shape. If you use petals, contrast them with another ingredient that is much larger in scale, such as a simple, curved, leaf shape, sticks of cinnamon and whole spices or chunks of wood bark. Yellow roses dry beautifully, retaining an excellent depth of colour and brightness. Use them with curls of lemon- or orange-peel and perhaps a few other yellow flowers such as coreopsis, sunflower petals, rudbeckia or wallflowers. For a more sophisticated version, combine yellow with pink roses and display the results against a background of pink or yellow.

The following recipes are suggestions for colour schemes and fragrances. Feel free to change and adapt the ingredients as you get more used to combining them to create your own recipes. Make batches of your favourite version to pack and give as presents.

WARMLY SCENTED POT-POURRI

Richly coloured, this pot-pourri is particularly pleasant to have around during the winter. A measure is based around a mug of about 260 millilitres (½ pint) capacity.

The image of pot-pourri is often tired, faded and dusty. Bright, clashing colours can bring it up to date. Here vivid Indian-yellow roses are displayed in a box lined with shocking-pink crêpe paper.

INGREDIENTS *(continued overleaf)*

5 measures deep-red rose petals or *whole rose-heads*

1 measure whole, dried, small sweet peppers

2 measures hibiscus flowers
1 measure dark-purple tulip,
    deep-red ranunculus,
    wallflower or peony petals
    or *whole flower-heads*
½ measure dried rose hips or
    red berries

½ measure whole nutmegs
1 measure spice and fixative
    mixture (see page 112)
cinnamon, rosewood and
    ginger essential oils

METHOD
Combine the dry ingredients then add the spice and fixative mixture. Add the essential oils, using 1 drop of each oil for each measure of dry ingredients. Put away to cure in paper bags for several weeks.

FESTIVE POT-POURRI

This pot-pourri smells of fruit, spice and all things Christmassy. Make plenty of it to fill the house at holiday time and to bag up to give away as gifts. The spice and fixative mixture given here is particularly spicy, and this recipe makes enough for several pot-pourris. It is always easier to make a spice and fixative mixture in reasonable quantities and it will keep well in a plastic bag or glass jar.

INGREDIENTS

3 measures dried, whole bay leaves

4 measures small whole pine cones

1 measure whole nuts in their shells, such as hazelnuts, pecans, almonds

1 measure dried, deep-red/ black hibiscus, mallow or *tulip petals*

1 measure dark-reddish-green, dried hydrangea florets

1 measure dried rose hips or *red berries*

10-12 cinnamon sticks

½ measure whole star anise

½ measure tonquin beans

1 measure dried orange-peel in curls

a selection of essential oils from cinnamon, orange or mandarin, clove, pine, myrrh

Spice and fixative mixture

100 grams (3½ ounces) ground orris root

100 grams (3½ ounces) ground cloves

125 grams (4½ ounces) ground cinnamon

50 grams (1¾ ounces) ground ginger

50 grams (1¾ ounces) allspice

50 grams (1¾ ounces) ground nutmeg

25 grams (1 ounce) brown sugar

25 grams (1 ounce) ground benzoin

25 millilitres (1 fluid ounce) brandy (optional)

METHOD

Mix all the main ingredients together, adjusting proportions to suit you. You could use dried fungi or wood bark rather than whole nuts in their shells or any of the exotic botanicals and seed pods available, to add shape and texture. Next add one measure of the spice and fixative mixture. When the fixative has been well mixed with the main ingredients add some essential oils. Use a blend of them all or highlight just two, such as orange and clove. In total use about 12 drops of oil for this amount of mixture. Put away to cure for as long as possible, but at least three weeks. Start making these pot-pourris well before Christmas if they are intended for use as gifts.

Extra textures and scent

Once you have discovered how to make dry pot-pourris and scented mixtures, you may want to search further afield to find more unusual ingredients. There are plenty to choose from. Anything that can be dried and will remain dried without changing or losing its

Home-made pot-pourri should look as good as it smells, even close-up. Making your own blends, such as this festive recipe, ensures that everything included is to your taste.

colour can be included. If it is scented, then so much the better as long as the fragrance will blend and combine with other scents. Avoid things with a dominating smell that will become too assertive in the final mixture.

A good place to begin looking for exciting things is among plant seeds and seed pods. Many of these occur as traditional cooking ingredients and spices, such as nutmeg and allspice. Many of the lily family of bulbs have large and attractive seed pods and so do several irises. *Iris foetidissima* has dramatic pods that burst open to reveal glossy orange berries and they dry very satisfactorily to use in potpourri. Tree seeds, such as acorns from oak, dry well and look neat and pretty mixed with other ingredients.

All the various pepper seeds are worth discovering. The little, red berries sold as pink peppercorns are actually the fruit of *Schinus molle*. They are often included in the ready-made packs of mixed peppercorns, which include pink, green, white and black varieties. Look out for long pepper too, which is quite different in appearance from the round peppercorns with which we are more familiar. Long pepper has stiff, catkin-shaped berries and was probably the original pepper to find its way from the East to the Mediterranean as early as the fourth century BC. It is used in North-African spice mixtures for cooking. Poppy seed heads from the species *Papaver somniferum* make an elegant addition to pot-pourri. They are only a nuisance if they are very ripe or split, shedding thousands of their tiny seeds everywhere. Be sure they have no little splits in the seed pod or, if they are so ripe that the spaces at the top of each section of the pod are open, shake out all the seeds and save them to sow in the garden for next year's crop before including them with other ingredients.

Fennel, caraway and angelica seeds are aromatic and pretty. As they are quite tiny, they are best used in small-scale mixtures where they will not simply disappear to the bottom. Cardamom pods are larger and a pretty pale-green when freshly dried. Mace is the outer lacy covering of the nutmeg seed. Its pale-orange colour and interesting shape make it a good ingredient to include in your potpourri repertoire. Oak moss is a lichen found growing on both live and dead wood. It is a pale silvery grey-green and looks beautiful mixed with many different colours. It has the ability to absorb other scents around it and was used in Edwardian days as a fixative in its own right for pot-pourris. It is pretty chopped quite small or in little clusters, rather like natural sponge. Leave it attached to its host – small twigs, bark or branches – for a larger-scale effect.

Bark and twigs, both exotic and found in the garden, have a useful place in pot-pourri. Cassia and cinnamon you can buy dried while anything you collect yourself will need to be dried carefully and cleaned up if necessary. Wood and bark are useful as they absorb oils and scents within the mixture. Wood shavings are often used in cheap and crude commercial pot-pourris. Garishly coloured and unpleasantly scented, they give pot-pourri a bad name. Natural wood shavings left uncoloured are a lovely addition, particularly

There are no limits to what you can add to a pot-pourri for texture as long as it lasts well. Collect natural debris from a woodland or seashore walk or buy textured ingredients such as dried fungi, seed pods and lichen.

from a scented wood such as cedarwood. Unless they are cut very small, they look best combined with other woody or earthy ingredients rather than delicate, coloured petals and flower-heads.

Small dried fungi are sold these days for flower arranging and decorative floristry and they add another element to certain pot-pourris. They are generally dark-brown, grey or black but often have pretty textures and a lovely surface sheen. Herbalists sell many different dried roots, stems and bark, chiefly designed for medicinal purposes and some of them make good ingredients for pot-pourris. You should be able to find calamnus root, angelica root – both natural fixatives – as well as vanilla pods, liquorice sticks, barberry and bayberry bark, oak bark, wild cherry bark, sandalwood raspings, casuarina pods, spikenard, galangal and many, many more.

FRAGRANCE AND LIGHT

Few of us need to rely on the light of candles these days. We now use them in a decorative rather than functional way and as a means to create atmosphere and drama. A further element can be added to candles in the form of scent. With the wider availability these days of pure essential oils all kinds of opportunities open up for creating fragrance as well as atmosphere.

The earliest lights were made from oils and waxes with a simple straw or reed wick dipped in them. This made a controlled, if faint and often spluttery flame, but would have given enough light for general tasks. These early lighting devices probably smelt unpleasant, depending on the source of the fuel used in them, as oils were not deodorized then and probably often came from animals. Beeswax is one natural wax that has always made excellent candles. It burns well and slowly and gives off a faint honey scent, which is delicious and soothing. Church candles, which need to burn steadily and long, have always been made from beeswax, but it is an expensive material for candles. Paraffin wax is much cheaper and commonly used these days for commercial candle making.

The early American settlers made fragrant candles from the wax obtained from a shrubby plant known as wax myrtle. The berries from the *Myrica cerifera* plant were boiled. Their waxy coating that floated to the surface was then reheated and made into little cakes, like night lights, which provided a white flame and a sweet scent when burning. Another plant of the same genus, *Myrica gale* or sweet gale, has similar properties, producing a balsam scent from the wax of the berries. The third member of this genus to be used for this purpose was held in such esteem that there were penalties for people who picked the berries before the given harvesting time. Bayberry or *Myrica pensylvanica* was the winter candle of Christmas in the early days of the American colonies and the distinctive scent, strongest just after the candle was snuffed out, spelt Christmas and festivities to the early settlers.

Making candles at home is quite an easy process but you will need some basic equipment to do the job properly. If you intend to start making candles so that you can have the shapes, colours and scents you want, go to the trouble of getting at least some proper moulds and a dipping can. You will also need to be aware of a few rules about the size of wick to diameter of candle and the need to add stearin to paraffin wax if you are going to make moulded, rather than dipped, candles. Perhaps most importantly, invest in a good instruction book (see Further Reading on page 157).

The first candles were probably made by the dipping process. A tall, narrow container, like a narrow saucepan, holds the molten wax. If you are doing this at home, you must be careful not to overheat the wax as it is flammable. It should ideally be maintained at a temperature of no more than 71°C (160° F). Into this a long piece of wick bent in half over a rod is dipped. The wick is dipped many times into the wax and withdrawn to cool and set between dips. Slowly the wax builds up around the wick and a characteristic tall, thin pair of slightly tapering candles are made. Colour can be added to the body of wax or it can be applied as a final dipping coat, leaving white wax underneath.

Candles seem to be back in fashion today and many of the thick pillar candles come ready-scented. Some are overpoweringly sweet and sickly but many of the best scents are sharp and clean, such as lemon, pine and lime. The best scented candles are those impregnated with scent. Adding drops of essential oil to the pool of molten wax around the wick of a wide candle does not really seem to be very effective though it does give a faint perfume. If you cannot find a ready-made scented candle to your liking, you will have to start to make your own. Adding the scent is very easy. All it means is putting drops of essential oil into the melted wax before pouring and moulding. Use about 25 to 35 drops to each 225 grams (8 ounces) of wax. You can use single fragrances or make your own blends. The

perfume from a good scented candle should smell quite strongly even before it is lit. The scent can be quite pervasive, lingering in fabrics and furnishings in a room well after the candle is finished, so be sure that you really like the scent you have chosen. If all this sounds too messy and complicated, the best solution is probably to stick with the twentieth century and use an electric light. You can buy little rings that sit above the bulb and hold essential oils. The warmth of the light makes the oils evaporate, giving off any scent you choose. There are even small, self-contained units powered by battery or mains electricity that do the same job.

Create atmosphere through colour and scent for winter festivities. Plain candles are an immediate way to set the right mood, while good, scented ones can make it even better.

QUICK AND EASY SCENTED GIFTS

This is the time of year to enjoy making use of your gardening efforts by turning the harvest into useful products and gifts. Even if you have to buy raw ingredients it is still satisfying to make them into something that simply could not be found in a shop and shows that you have taken time and trouble on someone else's behalf. Organized people plant bowls of winter bulbs to give as presents when the green spears are just pushing through the soil, fat with the promise of scented blooms. This means making a special effort to buy the bulbs at the right time and planting them sufficiently early

145

to give them long enough to develop. Alternatively, you can buy pots of ready-planted bulbs and add a personal, special touch by putting them into a better container than the one in which they came, and adding fresh, green moss and a jaunty ribbon bow.

There is no end to the variety of scented household gifts. Ideas include candles, polishes, cleaners, linen sachets, and lotions. To be practical, it is best to decide on one thing to make in quantity rather than trying to make a different gift for everyone. Put a day aside to make it and to pack and label the end results. This is far more fun and a lot less expensive than a day's shopping.

PERFUME POWDER

Use this perfume powder to fill small bags made from scraps of silk and finished with ribbon. Alternatively, put the powder into workaday linen or muslin sachets and pack several into a neat, wooden Shaker box or small, lidded basket for a more stylish presentation. Sachets and bags filled with this powder can be hung in cupboards and laid in drawers and desks. Making the powder is a pleasant process and will fill the house with fragrance. Using a pestle and mortar is the correct way to pound the ingredients but an electric spice or coffee grinder will make the job quicker if you prefer.

INGREDIENTS

50 grams (1¾ ounces) cloves

50 grams (1¾ ounces) nutmeg

50 grams (1¾ ounces) cinnamon

50 grams (1¾ ounces) caraway seed

50 grams (1¾ ounces) dried orange-peel

50 grams (1¾ ounces) tonka beans

300 grams (10½ ounces) orris root powder

METHOD

Grind or pound the cloves, cinnamon, caraway, orange-peel and tonka beans. Grate the nutmeg. Mix these together well and add the powdered orris root. The mixture can be quite coarse. Put into small fabric bags or sachets. Label these well and explain what they are and for what they are to be used if you are giving them as presents.

Bags or boxes of pot-pourri made from any of the recipes in this book would make a good gift, especially if you take the trouble to wrap and present the gift in an interesting way. If you want a simple means of wrapping then plain, clear cellophane always look good. Find the proper crackly kind that is used for food. Cling film looks dreadful and does nothing for what is inside it. Cut a big square of cellophane and heap the chosen amount of pot-pourri inside. Bring up all the edges and tie tightly to make a bundle, with the excess cellophane making a big frill at the top. Use ribbon or tape to secure and decorate the bundle.

If you grow plenty of one particular scented plant, such as lavender or rosemary, why not make a variety of lotions and potions from it during the summer months that can be put into small baskets and

Facility

22,500 square f
6 group study roo
70 computers
Over 300 seats
Audio and video
equipment
Restrooms
Photocopies

Reference Services

Librarian assistance in
person or by telephone
during all open hours.

Collection

Circulating books
(3 week loan period)
Reference books
Reference videotapes
Textbooks on reserve
Course reserve
  materials
Magazines
Newspapers
Large selection of
  electronic databases

Online

Access electronic
  resources
Check your library
  record
Renew books
Place a hold or request
  on books
LINK+ virtual Library
http://192.33.187.2521

Welcome to the new
Mission College Library

Please turn off cell
phones. No food or drink
in library (except water in
resealable bottles).

Hours
Mon.-Thurs. 10:00-
8:00pm
Friday 10:00-3:00pm
Saturday 11:00-3:00pm
Closed Sunday and
school holidays.

Reference Desk
408 855-5151
Circulation Desk
408 855-5150

Your student ID card is
your library card.

http://lib.wvmccd.cc.ca.us

given as presents later in the year? You might include a lavender bath essence, sachets filled with the dried flowers, a small lavender wreath made from twisted stems, a bundle of dried stems for burning on a fire, even some home-made lavender-scented candles.

If you have collected plenty of dried, scented flowers and foliage over the year but are unsure about how to use it, mix it with a spice and fixative mixture (see page 112) or the perfume powder (see page 101) and use it to fill small pillows and cushions, either home-made or bought. If your skills stretch to embroidery or appliqué, decorate a plain cushion with the name of the herb or flower or simply the word 'sleep'. Choose fabric patterns that are likely to fit in with any type of interior, such as small, geometric designs, stripes or homespun checks, or find old fabrics and lace to make antique-looking cushions for pretty bedrooms.

SCENTED GIFTS FOR GARDENERS

Thinking of gift ideas – to make or buy – is so much easier when someone has a special interest or enthusiasm. If you know a keen gardener, this gives you plenty of scope for inspiration. Here are a few suggestions for beautifully scented, practical gardening gifts.

There are books that will feed gardeners' enthusiasm and imagination and give them inspiration. Scent as a subject for gardening books has not been very widely covered but there are a few good modern books and some old classic ones still available second-hand if you search the right lists and bookshops.

Every gardener – even those with just a window box or a few pots on a terrace – would welcome a gift of some bulbs of scented plants. It is best to be generous and give plenty of one type rather than a few

By packing a basket with carefully chosen, scented gifts you can make a very personalized present. Keeping to a colour scheme or a theme, such as roses, makes the whole gift particularly stylish. Included here are rose-scented soaps and powder, a potted miniature rose shrub, rose-water and glycerine, and dried flowers.

147

of several, so that the display makes a bigger impact. Include a bag of potting compost or pebbles in which to plant the bulbs and perhaps even a new pot or bowl so that the recipient has everything he or she needs. Tulips, crocuses, narcissi, hyacinths and iris are all suitable, depending on the time of year you are giving the present. Some freesias are a good idea if you know that the gardener has a greenhouse or conservatory in which to grow them. For a gardener with more experience you could give something such as the tuberose *Polianthes* 'The Pearl', with its outstanding fragrance and double, white, tubular flowers; or, equally unusual and exotic, *Pancratium calathinum (Hymenocallis calathina)* or sea lily, with pure-white, fragrant flowers, which is happy in a conservatory or even outdoors in sheltered places. Eucharis grandiflora is another scented, white-flowered plant suitable for growing in a pot indoors or in a conservatory or greenhouse. Sometimes called Bethlehem lily, this little-known plant has clusters of daffodil-like flowers on straight stems above glossy, green, hosta-shaped leaves. You should be able to find all these bulbs in a large garden centre or nursery or by mail order from a specialist bulb-supplier. All the scented lilies make excellent gifts too, but make sure that the gift will be opened and used quite quickly before the bulbs dry out.

If you know a gardener's plans, you could supply a longed-for herb plant, scented shrub or a batch of small lavender bushes to make a hedge or path border. A small myrtle plant or little bay tree in a pot decorated with a ribbon bow will melt the hardest heart and a carefully trained jasmine or topiary herb, such as rosemary, shows that you have spent time achieving the result.

Soothing lotions and balms for rough, overworked skin are another good gift for a gardener. Flowers such as marshmallow, rose, elderflower and pot-marigold have been used traditionally to make creams and lotions to soothe sore and chapped skin that suffers from the drying effect of working with soil or the burning caused by exposure to the sun and wind. Ideally, make your own mixtures with home-grown herbs. Otherwise buy a good brand, decant to another container or remove the original label and add your own and attach a little bunch or sprig of an appropriate herb or flower. Then put it into a basket along with some other small, luxurious gifts. A home-made liqueur based on herbs or fruit would be delicious after a hard day's gardening. A batch of several different herb jellies made with a sharp apple base flavoured from your own herb and flower harvest and potted into very small jars would be a real treat. Some are good with meat and game while others make delicious sweet spreads for scones or toast. Scented sleep pillows might help a tired gardener to relax where strong doses of outdoor air have failed. A herb garland containing lots of different dried culinary herbs would scent the kitchen and be useful for instant bouquet garnis too. All these small gifts can be dressed up by wrapping them with style and presenting them in something useful, such as a garden basket, trug or good, hand-made terracotta pot.

Right. *Pack a gift basket for a gardening friend. Include soothing skin salve, efficient soap, a pair of sturdy gloves and perhaps an antique hyacinth glass or some old clay pots. Other ideas include herb jellies and home-made pot-pourri.*

Below. *Blazing-red tulips light up the garden like no other spring flower. A big bag of bulbs makes a perfect present for any gardener's borders or containers.*

SOOTHING HAND GEL

A cooling, non-sticky hand gel perfect to use after gardening.

INGREDIENTS

2 tablespoons glycerine
2 tablespoons powdered
  arrowroot

16 tablespoons elderflower
  water
6 drops sweet-orange essential
  oil

METHOD

Gently warm the glycerine in a double boiler or a bowl over a pan of boiling water. Add the arrowroot and stir until it is well mixed and has thickened. Pour in the elderflower water and stir until you have a clearish gel. Take it from the heat and leave to cool. Before potting into small jars add the essential oil and stir very thoroughly.

FORWARD PLANNING

Winter gives the gardener plenty of time to plan new projects, to order new plants and seeds and generally to get ready for when the weather allows a start to be made again.

If the ground is not frozen or covered in snow, the winter months are a good time to plant trees, shrubs and roses. After planting roses, cut back each branch by a third of its length to counteract any root damage caused in the upheaval of planting and to reduce the chance of movement caused by strong winds rocking the bush before it has had a chance to settle in and make new root growth. If your garden does not contain at least a couple of old-fashioned scented roses, order some now. There are plenty of small varieties to choose from for gardens too small to grow conventional, large, shrub roses. Another way to include more scented roses is to grow standard and semi-standard roses, which are simply bushes at the top of a single, straight stem, or to train climbing roses up pillars and frames. Training roses allows more space beneath them for other, smaller plants.

Take time during the quieter winter months to choose the best scented plants for your garden by reading catalogues and gardening books. It is often much easier to look through catalogues and send off for seeds from the warmth of an armchair than make a journey to a nursery and this is also a good way to compare all the different varieties on offer from various companies. More and more emphasis is now being put on fragrant varieties of plants. It is almost as if scent in the garden were a new discovery rather than an element that has been neglected for years. Your detective work will, hopefully, be interesting as well as useful. You may find out, for example, that a commonly grown shrub, such as philadelphus, has many species and varieties within the genus. The small-flowered, old-fashioned species *Philadelphus coronarius* has a powerfully strong scent, which carries on the air, but a less common type, such as *P. falconeri*,

which grows into a large bush, has hardly any scent. The smaller philadelphus varieties, such as the double 'Manteau d'Hermine' often recommended for small gardens, have a much fainter scent that *P. coronarius*. The rather dull leaves of these shrubs are unexciting for an important place in the garden so choose either the golden-leaved form *P. coronarius* 'Aureus', which keeps its fresh, bright-green colour all summer, or *P. coronarius* 'Variegatus', with its pretty cream-edged leaves. Another interesting area is the huge genus of lilacs or *Syringa*, which vary from type to type, some having more scent than others even within the same colour ranges. If you have little garden space but want to include a lilac or two, look out for some of the species and varieties such as *S. microphylla* 'Superba' or the larger but graceful *S. × × persica*.

With some research it would be possible to plan a complete garden that contains only scented plants. These strict limitations might lead to some inconsistencies and obvious gaps, particularly in the range of colours and the absence of whole plant families because they have no scent at all. It is, therefore, probably a better idea to plant a mixture of scented and unscented plants to offer the widest palette of colour and choice of form. The other approach is to plant a small area or special part of the garden exclusively with highly fragrant plants and to enjoy their perfume in a concentrated way. Much depends on the site and the soil, on climatic conditions and how much sun or shade your garden has.

Part of the greatest pleasure in winter is to dream of the summer season to come. Perhaps this year there will be armfuls of scented lilac with which to fill the house.

SCENTED POSIES

It is possible to make small, scented posies at any time of year. They make a perfect gift as well as an instant flower arrangement for the house. Many gardeners pride themselves on being able to pick a bunch of flowers from the garden on any day of the year, and if they include something highly scented then it is even more of an achievement.

Small bunches of flowers that can be carried in the hand are part of a long tradition of symbolism and a means of conveying unspoken messages. We use flowers to a certain degree these days to express what we cannot always say verbally. A bunch or posy of flowers given to someone might say, I send you sympathy, special thanks or love, or wishes that you will get well. Carrying a small posy of flowers centuries ago might have had a grimmer reason behind it. A tussie-mussie or small bunch of certain specific herbs, leaves and flowers, was held in the hand or attached to a belt to ward off disease and infection. Before people understood how diseases were spread they thought that 'evil odours' carried in the air were to blame. The scented posy was sniffed and supposed to supply protection. This may explain our instinct to sniff a small bunch of flowers in expectation of its perfume. It is appropriate, therefore, that a posy should contain something with a lovely fragrance.

The Victorians loved their scented posies and buttonholes of perfumed flowers. They usually made them neat and organized in the same way that they formalized their flower beds and gardens. Often framed in a ruff of decorative leaves or a paper frill or lace collar, the flowers within the posy were arranged in rings of single colours or flower varieties ranged round a central, perfect bloom. Little posyholders were invented, made from filigree metal and glass, to hold a small bunch and keep the ends of the stems in water.

A scented rose is a traditional starting point for a posy and it should be just opening out from the bud stage. When roses are not available, any fairly solid, roundish flower or a sprig of a flowering shrub could be the starting point for the bunch, or even a little cluster of berries or a poppy seed head. The only way to put together a posy is to make it in your hand so be sure to have all the flowers and leaves ready before starting to assemble it. It can be a dense, tightly packed arrangement or made much looser with space between the flowers. For traditional bridal posies the flower stems are wired so that each bloom can be moved into an exact position. This gives a very neat, formal effect, but is slow and fiddly to do. The flower stems in this kind of posy are bound where they join the wire with special waterproof tape, which holds in any moisture. Some flowers respond favourably to this treatment and last extremely well, such as spray carnations, chrysanthemums, stephanotis and some types of rose. The choice of such flowers is rather limited, however, which

Scented spring flowers fill a Victorian jug decorated with primulas. The mixture includes auriculas, cowslips, rosemary, primroses and blue omphalodes. For the most natural effect, make a posy of the flowers in your hand and then simply transfer this into the jug. Let the flowers settle then loosen them a little so that they are not crammed together.

IDEAS FOR SCENTED POSIES

Here are some suggestions for scented ingredients for small posies. The colour schemes will depend on your taste and what you have available. You can probably add many other unscented things just for their colour and variety.

SPRING	SUMMER	AUTUMN	WINTER
Hyacinths	Sweet Williams	Bouvardia	Tuberose
Freesias	Roses	Roses	Hyacinths
Lilacs	Pinks and carnations	Mint	Witch hazel
Viburnum	Honeysuckle	Myrtle	Daphnes
Primroses	Sweet peas	Gardenia	Rosemary
Violets	Stocks	Stephanotis	Freesias
Auriculas	Thyme	Jasmine	Mimosa
Lily-of-the-valley	Lavender	Michaelmas daisy	Winter viburnum
Genista	Marjoram	varieties	Mahonia
Iris varieties	Bergamot	Ageratum	*Iris unguicularis*
Narcissus varieties	Hyssop	Clematis varieties	Winter honeysuckle
	Marigolds	*Amaryllis belladonna*	Sarcoccoca
		Scented geraniums	

is why bridal bouquets in the past were often unimaginative in their choice of flowers. An unwired natural posy can be hand-held on a special occasion and then kept for several days in a container of water.

Before you begin to put the flowers together in your hand make sure that everything you are going to use – such as wire or rubber bands, and all the flowers – is spread out in front of you and within easy reach. Once you start making the posy you will only have one free hand. Do not worry about cutting the stems short until it is all finished. Simply add flowers to the bunch one by one, either mixing types at random or making a formal arrangement in coloured rings. Hold the bunch loosely and turn it as you go, building up the posy bit by bit. When the posy is about half the size you want, slide an elastic band round the stems or tie it with wire to hold everything together. Continue to add flowers and other materials and finish off the outer edge with something that gives good definition. You could use a pretty leaf such as ivy or fern, or evergreen myrtle which smells delicious when touched, or a ring of marjoram, sage or thyme for an aromatic herb scent. When the posy is finished, cut all the stems to the same length and secure the whole bunch with wire, string or elastic bands. Cover this up with a ribbon if you wish. Leave enough length of stem for a hand to hold it easily and for the posy to stand in water when its immediate purpose has been finished with.

A SELECTION OF THE BEST SCENTED PLANTS

The following lists are suggestions of useful and easy-to-grow
plants that all have one thing in common – fragrance.

ROSES

Rosa × *alba* Old-fashioned type,
possibly a hybrid between the Dog
Rose *R. canina* and the Damask
Rose *R. damascena*.
  'Celestial' ('Céleste'), Clear pink
  'Félicité Parmentier', Pale pink
  'Great Maiden's Blush', Pink
  'Königin von Dänemark', Deep
    pink

Rosa damascena **The Damask Rose**
  'De Rescht', Deep red
  'Gloire de Guilan', Clear pink
  'Ispahan', Clear pink
  'La Ville de Bruxelles', Rich pink
  'Madame Hardy', White
  'Madame Knorr' ('Comte de
    Chambord'), Deep pink

Rosa gallica **The French Rose.**
Probably the oldest varieties of
garden roses.
  'Belle de Crécy', Light crimson
  'Belle Isis', Flesh pink
  'Cardinal de Richelieu', Dark
    purple
  'Charles de Mills', Deep red/
    purple
  'Officinalis', Crimson pink
  'Président de Sèze' ('Jenny
    Duval'), Violet/purple/grey
  'Rosa Mundi', Striped white and
    crimson
  'Tuscany Superb', Deep crimson

Rosa × *centifolia* **The Provence
Rose.** Clear pink
  'Fantin-Latour', Pink
  'Juno', Blush pink
  'Muscosa' (Moss Rose)
    'Maréchal Davoust', Carmine
    'Mousseline', Blush pink
    'Old Pink Moss', Pink
    'William Lobb', Dark crimson
  'Parvifolia' ('Burgundy Rose'),
    Deep pink/claret
  'Paul Ricault', Rose pink
  'Petite de Hollande', Pale pink
  'Robert le Diable', Purple/grey
  'Tour de Malakoff', Magenta/
    violet

Bourbon and Hybrid Perpetual
Roses
  'Adam Messerich', Pink

'Baron Girod de l'Ain', Dark
  crimson
'Baronne Adolph de Rothschild',
  Deep pink
'Boule de Neige', White
'Bourbon Queen', Pink
'Commandant Beaurepaire',
  Striped pink/purple/red
'Empereur du Maroc', Maroon
'Ferdinand Pichard', Striped pink/
  purple
'Georg Arends', Clear pink
'Gloire de Ducher', Crimson
'Honorine de Brabant', Pink,
  striped crimson/mauve
'La Reine Victoria', Warm pink
'Louise Odier', Pink
'Madame Isaac Pereire', Crimson
'Madame Lauriol de Barny', Pale
  pink
'Madame Pierre Oger', Shell pink
'Souvenir de la Malmaison', Blush
  pink
'Souvenir du Docteur Jamain',
  Maroon

Hybrid Musk Roses
  'Buff Beauty', Apricot
  'Cornelia', Coppery-pink
  'Daybreak', Yellow
  'Felicia', Silvery pink
  'Francesca', Apricot/yellow
  'Moonlight', Creamy white
  'Pax', Creamy white
  'Penelope', Pink
  'Prosperity', White
  'Vanity', Deep pink

Modern Shrub Roses
  Charles Austin, Apricot
  'Frühlingsanfang', Ivory
  'Frühlingsgold', Pale yellow
  'Golden Chersonese', Golden
    yellow
  'Golden Wings', Yellow
  Graham Thomas, Yellow
  Heritage, Shell pink
  Hilda Murrell, Pink
  'Magenta', Magenta/mauve
  'Pretty Jessica', Warm pink
  'The Reeve', Deep pink
  'The Squire', Crimson
  'The Wife of Bath', Pink
  Wise Portia, Purple

Japanese or Rugosa Roses
  'Agnes', Yellow
  'Blanc Double de Coubert', White
  'Conrad Ferdinand Meyer', Pink
  'Mrs Anthony Waterer', Crimson
  'Roseraie de l'Haÿ', Crimson
  'Sarah van Fleet', Clear pink

Species and Climbing Species Roses
Rosa californica 'Plena', Deep pink
Rosa dupontii, White
Rosa eglantaria The Sweetbriar, Pale
  pink. Scented foliage
  'Amy Robsart', Pink
  'Greenmantle', Red with white eye
  'Janet's Pride', Pink/white
  'Julia Mannering', Pale pink
  'Lady Penzance', Salmon pink
  'Lord Penzance', Yellow
  'Meg Merilees', Crimson
Rosa gentiliana, Cream (rambler)
Rosa macrantha, Blush pink
Rosa moschata The Autumn Musk
  Rose, White (rambler)
Rosa pimpinellifolia
  (*R. spinosissima*) The Scotch Rose,
  Creamy white
  'Stanwell Perpetual', Blush pink
Rosa primula, Yellow. Scented
  foliage
Rosa rubus, White (rambler)
Rosa setipoda Clear pink/white
Rosa wichuraiana, White (rambler)

Climbing Roses
  'Aimée Vibert', Pure white
  'Alchymist', Yellow
  'Blush Noisette', Mauve/pink
  'Céline Forestier', Pale yellow
  'Climbing Château de Clos-
    Vougeot', Deep crimson
  'Climbing Crimson Glory', Deep
    crimson
  'Climbing Etoile de Hollande',
    Deep crimson
  'Climbing Josephine Bruce',
    Crimson
  'Climbing Lady Hillingdon',
    Apricot/yellow
  'Climbing Lady Sylvia', Blush
    pink
  'Climbing Madame Abel
    Châtenay', Blush pink
  'Climbing Mrs Herbert Stevens',

White
'Climbing Souvenir de la
 Malmaison', Blush pink
'Dreamgirl', Peach
'Elegance', Lemon yellow
'Gloire de Dijon', Buff/apricot
'Gruss an Teplitz', Crimson
'Guinée', Dark red
'Kathleen Harrop', Pale pink
'Lady Waterlow', Pink
'Lawrence Johnston', Yellow
'Le Rêve', Pale yellow
'Leverkusen', Lemon yellow
'Madame Alfred Carrière', Pale pink
'Madame Grégoire Staechelin', Clear
 pink
'Maigold', Warm yellow
'Maréchal Niel', Pale yellow
'Paul's Lemon Pillar', Pale lemon
 yellow
'Souvenir de Claudius Denoyel',
 Crimson
'Zéphirine Drouhin', Deep pink

Rambling Roses
'Albéric Barbier', Cream
'Albertine', Coppery pink
'Alexandre Girault', Deep pink
'Blush Rambler', Blush pink
'Bobbie James', White
'Emily Gray', Warm yellow
'Frances E. Lester', Apple blossom
 pink
'François Juranville', Coral pink
'Goldfinch', Pale yellow
'Kew Rambler', Rose pink
'Paul's Himalayan Musk', Blush
 pink
'Paul Transon', Apricot
'Rambling Rector', Creamy white
'Sanders' White Rambler', White
'Seagull', White
'The Garland', Creamy peach
'Veilchenblau', Magenta/lilac
'Wedding Day', Creamy white

Modern Climbing Roses
Good grown as pillar roses and
usually repeat-flowering.
'Aloha', Copper/pink
'Compassion', Apricot
'Copenhagen', Scarlet
Coral Dawn, Coral pink
Highfield, Yellow
'New Dawn', Silver pink
'Parade', Carmine pink
'White Cockade', White

**Hybrid Tea and Floribunda Bush
Roses**
Red Shades
Alec's Red, Red
'Crimson Glory', Crimson
'Dusky Maiden', Crimson
Fragrant Cloud, Scarlet
Mister Lincoln, Deep crimson
Papa Meilland, Crimson

Red Devil, Scarlet
Velvet Fragrance, Crimson
'Wendy Cussons', Light red

Yellow Shades
'Arthur Bell', Yellow
Chinatown, Yellow
'Dutch Gold', Golden yellow
Mountbatten, Lemon yellow
Pot o' Gold, Yellow
'Sutter's Gold', Peach/yellow

White Shades
'Evening Star', Pure white
Iceberg, White
Margaret Merril, Blush/white
'White Wings', White

Pink and Apricot Shades
'Apricot Nectar', Apricot/pink
'Apricot Silk', Apricot
'Café', Coffee
Elizabeth of Glamis, Salmon pink
Escapade, Pale pink
Grace de Monaco, Warm pink
'Home Sweet Home', Clear pink
Just Joey, Copper
'La France', Pale pink
Mischief, Salmon pink
'Ophelia', Blush pink
'Prima Ballerina', Clear pink
Pristine, Blush pink
Silver Jubilee, Pink/apricot
Whisky Mac, Copper

Lilac Shades
Blue Moon, Lilac
Blue Parfum, Lilac
'Great News', Lilac/purple

SWEET PEAS *Lathyrus odoratus*
*Be guided by catalogues and choose
those varieties marked as having
good fragrance. Look out for old-
fashioned scented mixtures, too.*
'Andrew Unwin', Lavender
'Charles Unwin', Pink on lemon
'Cream Southbourne', Cream
'Fiona', Salmon pink
'Hunter's Moon', Cream
'Leamington', Mauve
'Maggie May', Blue/white
'Nancy Colledge', Cerise/salmon
'North Shore', Deep blue
'Old Times', Cream/flushed blue
'Pennine Floss', Cerise
'Pink Bouquet', Salmon pink
'Red Ensign', Scarlet
'Rosy Frills', White/pink edged
'Royal Baby', Lavender
'Royal Wedding', Pure white
'The Doctor', Mauve
'White Supreme', White

ANNUALS
*Plants sown from seed and flowering
in the same season.*
Alyssum 'Rosie O'Day', Deep pink

Asperula azurea-setosa, Lavender
 blue
Calendula officinalis (Pot-marigold),
 Orange
Centaurea moschata (Sweet sultan)
 'Dairy Maid', Cream
 'The Bride', White
Gilia tricolor, Blue/gold/purple
Heliotropium × *hybridum*, Lilac/
 purple
Lathyrus odoratus (Sweet pea)
 see separate list
Layia elegans (Tidy tips), Yellow/
 white
Malcolmia maritima (Virginian
 stock), Pink and white
Matthiola bicornis (Night-scented
 stock), Mauve, cream
M. incana (Ten-week stock), Pink,
 red, white, cream
Mirabilis jalapa (Marvel of Peru),
 Red, yellow, white, pink
Nicotiana affinis (Tobacco plant)
 'Fragrant Cloud', White
 'Sensation Mixed', Mixed colours
N. sylvestris, White
Ocimum basilicum (Basil), Purple or
 green leaves
Reseda odorata (Mignonette), Lime
 green
Zaluzianskya ovata (Night phlox),
 White and maroon

BIENNIALS
*Plants grown from seed in one season
and which flower in the following
season.*
Cheiranthus cheiri (Wallflower),
 Mixed colours
Dianthus barbatus (Sweet William),
 Reds, pinks, crimson
D. 'Sweet Wivelsfield', Mixed
 colours
Hesperis matronalis (Sweet rocket),
 White and mauve

**INDOOR, CONSERVATORY
AND GREENHOUSE PLANTS**
Acacia dealbata (Mimosa), Yellow
Chlidanthus fragrans, Pale yellow
 (bulb)
Datura (Angel's trumpet), White,
 mauve
Epacris, Pale pink
Eucalyptus citriodora, Lemon-
 scented foliage
Eucharis amazonica, White (bulb)
Freesia × *kewensis*, Mixed colours
 (corm)
Gardenia jasminoides, White
Hoya bella, Blush white
H. carnosa, Pinkish-white (climber)
Plumeria rubra (Frangipani), Pink,
 red, white, yellow
Stephanotis floribunda, White
 (climber)

155

TREES, SHRUBS, CLIMBERS, HERBACEOUS PERENNIALS, BULBS

T = Tree, S = Shrub, Cl = Climber, P = Herbaceous Perennial, B = Bulb

Angelica archangelica (Angelica), All parts aromatic P

Anthemis nobilis (Common chamomile), Foliage and flowers aromatic P

Aquilegia fragrans (Columbine), White or purple P

A. viridiflora, Green P

Artemisia abrotanum (Southernwood; Lad's love), Aromatic foliage P

A. dracunculus (Tarragon), Aromatic foliage P

Azalea see *Rhododendron*

Azara microphylla, White S

Buddleia alternifolia, Mauve S

B. crispa, Pink S

B. davidii (Butterfly bush), Purple S

B. fallowiana, Lavender, white S

Buxus sempervirens (Common box), Aromatic foliage S

Catalpa bignonioides (Indian bean tree), White S/T

Ceanothus × 'Gloire de Versailles', Powder blue S

Cedrus atlanticus (Atlantic cedar), Aromatic foliage T

Chamaecyparis (Cypress), Aromatic foliage T

Chimonanthus praecox (Winter sweet), Ivory/yellow S

Clematis armandii, White Cl

C. cirrhosa, Greenish-yellow Cl

C. flammula, White Cl

C. × *jouiniana*, Azure blue P

C. rehderiana, Yellow Cl

Convallaria majalis (Lily of the valley), White P

Corylopsis pauciflora, Pale yellow S

Crataegus laevigata (Hawthorn), White or pink T

Crocus laevigatus, White/purple B

Cytisus battandieri (Broom), Yellow S

Daphne blagayana, White S

D. × *burkwoodii*, Pale pink S

D. cneorum (Garland flower), Deep pink S

D. laureola (Spurge laurel), Green S

D. mezereum (Mezereon), Purple, white S

D. odora, Pink S

Dianthus × *allwoodii* (Pink), Pink, crimson, deep red, white, cream P

D. caryophyllus (Carnation; clove pink)
    Many hybrids and varieties, Mixed colours P

D. plumarius (Pink), Mixed colours P

Eucalyptus
    Many varieties, Aromatic foliage T/S

Eucryphia × *nymansensis* 'Nymansay', White S

Filipendula hexapetala, White P

Foeniculum vulgare (Fennel), Aromatic foliage P

Hamamelis mollis (Chinese witch hazel), Yellow T/S

Hyacinthoides non-scripta (English bluebell), Blue B

Hyacinthus orientalis (Hyacinth), Mixed colours B
    'Borah Multi-Flowered', Pink, blue, white B

Hyssopus officinalis (Hyssop), Purple, Aromatic foliage P

Iris florentina, Pale lilac P

I. pseudacorus (Yellow flag), Yellow P

I. reticulata, Purple B

I. unguicularis (Algerian iris), Mauve P

Itea ilicifolia, Greenish-white S

Jasminum officinale (Common white jasmine), White Cl

J. polyanthum, Blush white Cl

J. × *stephanense*, Pink Cl

Juniperus communis (Common juniper), Fragrant foliage T

Lavandula dentata (Lavender), Purple S

L. spica (Old English lavender), Purple, pink, white, mauve S

L. stoechas (French lavender), Purple S

Lilium auratum (Golden-rayed lily), White, spotted B

L. candidum (Madonna lily), White B

L. longiflorum (Easter lily), White B

L. regale, White B

L. wallichianum, White B

Lippia citriodora (Lemon-scented verbena), White. Fragrant foliage S

Lonicera caprifolium (Honeysuckle), Cream Cl

L. etrusca, Cream Cl

L. fragrantissima, Cream S

L. × *italica*, Yellow/pink Cl

L. japonica (Japanese honeysuckle), Cream Cl

L. periclymenum (Woodbine), Cream Cl

L. × *purpusii*, Cream S

Magnolia grandiflora, Cream T/S

Melissa officinalis (Lemon balm), Fragrant foliage P

Mentha × *gentilis* (Mint), Fragrant foliage P

M. × *piperita*, Fragrant foliage P

M. pulegium, Pungent foliage P

M. rotundifolia (Apple mint), Fragrant foliage P

M. spicata (Spearmint), Fragrant foliage P

Monarda didyma (Bergamot), Red, pink P

Myrtus communis (Common myrtle), White. Fragrant foliage S

Narcissus (Narcissus; Daffodil), Many varieties, Yellow, white B

Nepeta × *faassenii* (Catmint), Mauve. Aromatic foliage P

Oenothera biennis (Evening primrose), Yellow P

Origanum majorana (Sweet marjoram), Pink. Aromatic foliage P

O. vulgare (Common marjoram), Pink. Aromatic foliage P

Paeonia lactiflora (Paeony), Pink, red P

Pelargonium
    Many varieties, Aromatic foliage S

Philadelphus (Mock orange)
    Many varieties, White S

Pinus (Pine)
    Many varieties, Resinous/aromatic T

Primula
    Hybrids, Mixed colours P

P. auricula, Mixed colours P

P. veris (Cowslip), Yellow P

P. vulgaris (Primrose), Pale yellow P

Rhododendron auriculatum, White S

R. brevistylum, Aromatic foliage S

R. callimorphum (*R. cyclium*), Pink S

R. glaucophyllum, Scented foliage S

Rosmarinus officinalis (Rosemary), Mauve. Aromatic foliage S

Salvia officinalis (Sage), Aromatic foliage S

S. rutilans (Pineapple sage), Aromatic foliage P

Santolina incana, Yellow. Aromatic foliage S

Sedum roseum (Rose root), Purple P

Styrax japonica, White T

Thuya
    Many varieties, All parts aromatic T

Thymus (Thyme)
    Many varieties, Pink, mauve. Aromatic foliage P

Tilia (Lime; linden), Green T

Trachelospermum jasminoides, White Cl

Tulipa 'Black Parrot', Purple B

T. sylvestris, Yellow B

Ulex europaeus (Gorse), Yellow S

Verbena × *hybrida* 'Grandiflora', Mixed colours P

Viburnum × *bodnantense*, Pink S

V. × *burkwoodii*, Pink S

V. × *carlcephalum*, Pink S

V. carlesii, Pink S

V. fragrans, Pink S

Viola odorata (Sweet violet), White, purple P

FURTHER READING

Constable, David. *Candle Making,* Tunbridge Wells, Search Press, 1992

Fish, Margery. *Cottage Garden Flowers,* Newton Abbot, David & Charles, 1970

Genders, Roy. *Perfume in the Garden,* London, The Garden Book Club, 1954

Genders, Roy. *The Cottage Garden and Old-fashioned Flowers,* London, Pelham, 1983

Genders, Roy. *The Scented Flora of the World,* St Albans, Herts., Mayflower/Granada, 1977

Guyton, Anita. *The Natural Beauty Book,* London, Thorsons, 1991

Heriteau, Jacqueline. *Potpourris and Other Fragrant Delights,* London, Penguin Books, 1978

Houdret, Jessica. Pomanders, Posies and Pot-Pourri, Aylesbury, Shire Publications, 1988

Leyel, Mrs C. F. *Herbal Delights,* London, Faber & Faber, 1937

Lloyd, Christopher and Rice, Graham. *Garden Flowers from Seed,* London, Viking, 1991

McLean, Teresa. *Medieval English Gardens,* London, William Collins, 1981

Newdick, Jane. *Period Flowers,* London, Letts, 1991

Ohrbach, Barbara Milo. *The Scented Room,* London, Sidgwick & Jackson, 1986

Thomas, Graham Stuart. *The Old Shrub Roses,* London, Dent, 1979

Tolley, Emelie and Mead, Chris. *Herbs: Gardens, Decorations, and Recipes,* London, Sidgwick & Jackson, 1985

SUPPLIERS

UK
Seeds for herbs, vegetables, and annual, biennial and perennial flowers are available from nurseries and garden centres. They can also be purchased directly from these suppliers:

Chiltern Seeds, Bortree Stile, Ulverston, Cumbria LA12 7PB (Many unusual varieties.)

Johnson Seeds, Boston, Lincs. PE21 8AD

Suffolk Herbs, Monk's Farm, Pantlings Lane, Kelvedon, Essex CO5 9PG (Good for wildflower seeds.)

Suttons Seeds Ltd, Hele Road, Torquay, Devon TQ2 7QJ

Thompson and Morgan (Ipswich) Ltd, Poplar Lane, Ipswich, Suffolk IP8 3BU

Unwins Seeds, Mail Order Department, Histon, Cambs. CB4 4ZZ (Good for sweet peas.)

Roses are widely available from local nurseries and garden centres but the following nurseries have a particularly large selection:

David Austin Roses, Bowling Green Lane, Albrighton, Wolverhampton WV7 3HB (Comprehensive choice of old-fashioned varieties and English roses.)

Peter Beales Roses, London Road, Attleborough, Norfolk NR17 1AY

R Harkness and Co. Ltd, The Rose Garden, Hitchin, Herts. SG4 0JT

Wax and candle-making kits, moulds etc are available from craft shops or from:

Candle Maker's Supplies, 28 Blythe Road, London W14 0PP

USA
Roses of Yesterday and Today, Inc., 802 Brown's Valley Road, Watsonville, CA 95076

The Herb Cottage, c/o Washington National Cathedral, Mount Saint Alban, North-west Washington DC 20016

Thompson & Morgan (Seeds), PO Box 1308, Jackson, New Jersey 08527

AUSTRALIA
Berrima Lavender Farm, Market Place, Berrima, NSW 2577

Ross Roses, St Andrew's Terrace, Willunga, South Australia 5172

Buda Historic Home and Garden Plant Nursery, Corner Hunter & Urquhart Streets, Castlemaine, Victoria 3450

INDEX

ACKNOWLEDGEMENTS

Editor Michele Turney
Art Director Elaine Partington
Designer Nigel Partridge
Proof-reader and Indexer Peter Moloney
Production Hazel Kirkman and Charles James

Unless specified below,
the photographs for this book have been taken by Pia Tryde.

Liz Eddison: p.73
John Glover, Garden Picture Library: p.117
Clive Nichols: pp. 73, 120-1, 123, 124, 125
May Woods, Garden Picture Library: p. 116